With man[?]
fr a most delightful
weekend! (wish
you'd been with us —)
Affectionately
D.

November 1972

UPON THIS ROCK

UPON THIS ROCK

TEXT BY

AUBREY MENEN

Saturday Review Press

NEW YORK

Published simultaneously in Canada by
Doubleday Canada Ltd., Toronto

Library of Congress Catalog Card Number: 70-154264

ISBN 0-8415-0193-9

Saturday Review Press
230 Park Avenue
New York, New York 10017

Printed in the United States of America

DESIGN BY TERE LOPRETE

CONTENTS

UPON THIS ROCK

I

CORONATION

When I first saw St. Peter's, like a great number of people on their initial visit, I did not like it very much. The dome was fine: but the inside of the church seemed too ornate. It would do better, it seemed to me, as a royal palace. There was even a huge throne at the end, ready for the monarch.

I was being shown around by a priest from the Vatican. I remember that he said the basilica was so big that Notre Dame in Paris could easily be fitted inside it. I thought that this might be a good idea: it would add a spiritual tone to the place, which I found distinctly lacking.

The truth was that I was ignorant, and it did not occur to me to be otherwise. After all, one does not have to know anything about Notre Dame to enjoy it. One just walks inside. I thought I could do the same with St. Peter's, but I was mistaken.

That was twenty years ago. Since then I have lived in Rome. I have got to know St. Peter's stone by stone. I have learned about the extraordinary men who put those stones together. As a result, I have come to look upon St. Peter's as one of the most fascinating and beautiful monuments in Western civilization.

St. Peter's cannot be understood by merely walking around it. It must be read, like a book. In what follows, I aim to help the visitor to do that, and since St. Peter's is the Pope's own church, I shall begin with him.

One morning in 1958 a monsignor from the Vatican rang my doorbell and with much ceremony handed me a large card with my name written on it. It was an invitation to be present at the coronation of "His Holiness John XXIII."

In fact I knew that no cards were necessary: Popes are crowned on a balcony in full view of everybody who cares to walk to St. Peter's Square. But before that took place, the new Pope would go through a ceremony that would roll back through the entire history of the Catholic Church. So I went.

When I arrived the great church was only half-lit. Twenty thousand people filled every cranny of it, and a murmur of voices rose to the arches of the roof and softly echoed, making a sound like surf upon a shore. The great of the earth were all around me, some in uniforms gleaming with gold braid. Few people

From the memorial of John XXIII in the Chapel of the Presentation (Emilio Greco, 1963)

looked at them. The church was so big that many of us had brought binoculars. These were focused on a little group of men and women, plainly, and even cheaply, dressed. They were the family of the man we were to see crowned: simple peasants, as he had once been, and looking pale and nervous. We stared at them because they were living symbols that the Papacy is the most democratic institution in the world. Anybody can become Pope. Anybody and even a nobody: once, in the Middle Ages, the whole college of cardinals had clambered, breathless, up a mountain, to kneel at the feet of an obscure hermit and tell the astonished old man they had chosen him to be the head of the Catholic Church.

The lights went up and St. Peter's became, upon the instant, a blaze of gold and precious marbles. Far away down the basilica, trumpeters sounded a fanfare. A choir began to sing an anthem. "Thou art Peter" they sang to a rather stout man who had just entered the basilica, swaying on a throne that was carried on the shoulders of bearers in red uniforms. He was not Peter. He was Angelo Roncalli, son of Giovanni Battista Roncalli and his wife Marianna, who had borne her husband ten children. The man on the throne was now known as John, a Pope, and the twenty-third of that name. But "Thou art Peter" sang the choir and I shall show why.

The Pope was surrounded by his court, dressed in a strange medley of costumes. Some wore Victorian dress, others were dashingly Renaissance, while the cardinals wore the great copes of medieval times. One man carried the Pope's tiara on a velvet cushion. It was strangely shaped. It looked like a tall, conical hat, bedizened with three crowns, one above another, glittering with jewels.

Midway down the church the procession was halted. A courtier raised a rod. On it was some burning flax. Flax burns very quickly. As it did so, the courtier thrust it toward the new Pope and intoned the words "*Sic transit gloria mundi*": "Thus passes worldly glory."

The procession arrived at the middle of the church. The throne was lowered. The Pope got down. He was dressed like a bishop, like any other bishop robed to say Mass, with a golden mitre on his head. He walked to the end of the basilica followed by cardinals, bishops, and abbots. He came to where there is the great bronze throne, ingeniously placed so that it seems to be floating in the air. He sat beneath it, on another throne, under a scarlet canopy. His cardinals, one by one, approached him and did him obeisance. They kissed his hand. Then came the bishops. They kissed his knee. Then the abbots, who kissed his slipper.

He read an address. Then he rose and walked to the very middle of the basilica. Here was a huge canopy supported by four twisted columns. Under this was an altar. He sang Mass, and when he lifted the Sacrament during the Elevation, there were tears in his eyes.

The Mass being over, the Pope once more moved in a glittering procession down the church. We, the privileged ones with tickets, had played our parts in the ceremony. It was now the turn of the people. I left the basilica and joined the crowd that filled the square outside. The spectators were largely made up of Romans.

The Pope appeared on a balcony in the middle of the façade. After a few sentences in Latin, a cardinal took the tiara from its velvet cushion, raised it high so that we all could see it, and placed it on the Pope's head. The new Pope, in the name of the Father, the Son, and the Holy Ghost, gave us all his benediction, and disappeared into the basilica. The crowd had watched the crowning in a judicious silence.

Let us go back to the beginning of the ceremony and study the meaning of each part of it.

The tiara was strangely shaped because the Papacy was founded at the time of the Roman Empire, and the Roman Emperors wore a tall, conical hat as a sign of their supremacy. The Popes considered themselves the Emperor's equal, and often his superior. Some even read the monarch lectures. The Emperors frequently lost their tempers and one went so far as to arrest a Pope and have him brought to the court in chains. But the Emperors have gone. The Pope remains. The man on the portable throne had just been

8

The main nave from above

elected to the oldest continuous high office in the history of the Western world.

His courtiers were witness of it. Their costumes spanned the centuries. They seemed to be dressed for a historical pageant, and so they were. It was a pageant meant to be looked at.

That is why they went down the whole length of the huge nave; and the nave was made so that it could hold a vast concourse of people. When the present basilica was first designed, the nave was much smaller. But before it could be built, the number of Catholics had greatly increased. So the nave was made as big as possible without ruining the design (though some say that is just what it did). St. Peter's is the biggest church in the world for the simple reason that it was built to show the Pope in his glory to as many people as possible, in flesh and blood and practically at arm's length. There is a charming custom that shows this. A Catholic can buy in the shops in Rome a white skullcap such as Popes wear. He can hold it out as the Pope goes by, and sometimes the Pope will take off his own skullcap, give it to the donor, and put the new one on his head.

But the Pope is, after all, just a priest. At some time in his life he will probably have been in charge of a parish. The man on the portable throne that I saw had been a humble army chaplain. That is why the procession is stopped, the flax burned, and the throne is lowered to the ground.

The next part of the ceremony plunges deeper into history, to the very beginning of the Church.

The Pope is dressed, as we have seen, as a bishop. The earliest Popes, in the first century after the crucifixion, did not call themselves by that name. They were simply bishops elected by the tiny Christian community of Rome, just as the cardinals began by being parish priests of the churches in the city. The early Popes did not claim to be the head of the whole Church, and some communities, such as that of Antioch, vigorously protested that they were not.

The first bishop of Rome was St. Peter and St. Peter was accepted by all as being the leader among the disciples of Jesus. Because of this the bishop of Rome could claim a very special authority, provided that he stood in direct succession to St. Peter, without a break.

The Pope, in his coronation ceremony, dramatically claims that he is just such a successor. He sits beneath the great gold floating throne. Inside this is the chair on which, it is claimed, St. Peter once sat. From here he goes to the altar in the middle of the church. Deep down underneath the altar is the tomb of the first of the Apostles. When the Pope raised the Sacrament, the grave of St. Peter was down below him.

That is why the choir had sung "Thou art Peter." The *first* bishop of Rome reposed beneath Angelo Roncalli's feet. He was the two hundred and sixty-second. The whole great church was built to make this clear.

He was crowned, not on his throne, nor at the altar, but on a balcony, in full sight of the Roman people. That also had its

reason. For centuries it was the people of Rome who chose the successor to their first bishop. They fought in the streets over the rival candidates and a Papal election often called forth rivers of blood. The tumults were so great that the system was changed. The Pope was elected by the cardinals sitting in the conclave. But even then the people of Rome sometimes had their way. Once, in the Middle Ages, when they thought the cardinals would elect a foreigner, they took the roof off the hall in which the cardinals were meeting, and menacing them with death, they bawled continuously, "Give us a Roman Pope."

It was all much quieter with Angelo Roncalli. But the Romans still feel that the Popes are theirs. They watched John crowned in silence because they did not know him. They were reserving their judgment.

The Pope, then, is an ordinary Christian elevated above the rest because of one single fact—he follows, in unbroken succession, St. Peter. Why, then, is Peter so important? Why is he considered so vital a figure among the men who knew Christ that this vast structure has been built over his tomb?

13

The Chair of St. Peter (Gian Lorenzo Bernini, 1666)

II

PETER

The Gospels contain some brilliantly done portraits, including one of Pontius Pilate which is worthy of Tacitus. But they are very vague about most of the disciples. Matthew is interesting before he was called. He is a tax-gatherer for the conquering Romans and heartily despised for it. He introduces Jesus to the company of publicans and sinners, but then he fades away into no more than a name. John is the beloved disciple, but if it is he who wrote the Gospel that goes under his name, he is remarkably self-effacing. Of Andrew we know very little except that he was a fisherman who introduced his brother to Jesus. But it is precisely that brother who is the exception to the rule. The Gospels speak more about Simon called Peter than any other one person save Jesus. He comes out from the pages as a real person, sometimes devoted, sometimes disloyal, sometimes obedient, sometimes exasperatingly argumentative—in other words, a man of deeply human character. Perhaps it was this that attracted Jesus to him and made him place him above all the other followers.

The Bible calls him "ignorant," by which it means he could not read and write. But he was by no means simple-minded. He was, in the first place, very firmly Jewish. He held to the rules and prohibitions of his religion but he went beyond mere conformism. He also believed in that most elusive doctrine to be found in the Hebrew prophets, namely, that a Messiah would come to save the Jews. They needed saving. Not only were they under the heel of the Romans: their masters disliked them. As a rule the Romans cared little about what their subjects believed as long as they paid their taxes. But with the Jews, they went out of their way to offend their faith. When Jesus began his teaching, this had produced a simmering of rebellion, especially in Galilee, that was later, after his death, to burst into a full (and disastrous) revolt. The ignorant fisherman shared the rebels' feelings, but he was not a man for armed rebellion. He believed God would solve the problem of the Jews. He awaited the Messiah.

When his brother brought him to Jesus, he immediately joined the little band of followers. We can measure the depth of

Consigning of the keys, from mural in the Sistine Chapel (Perugino, 1482)

LEFT *Head of Peter; mosaic in the crypt of St. Peter's*

his feelings at that moment by the simple fact that he gave up his livelihood, and left his family with two breadwinners the less.

Now, the other disciples willingly accepted Jesus as a prophet. They were slower to believe him to be the Messiah. But for Jesus to succeed in his mission it was vital that they should. He foresaw his own death: time was getting short. One day he put the question to them. He asked them who they thought him to be.

It was Peter who said, "Thou art the Anointed One": in other words, the Messiah. It was a turning point in the history of the world, for Jesus, in his turn, said, "Thou art Peter and upon this rock I will build my church, and the gates of Hell will not prevail against it."

Jesus went on to make his meaning clear. "I will give thee the keys of the kingdom of the heavens, and whatsoever thou shalt bind on earth shall be bound in the heavens, and whatsoever thou shalt loose on earth shall be loosed in the heavens."

They are momentous words and they repay study. In the first place, Jesus had called Peter "The Rock" (Cephas) on his very first meeting with him, a remarkable prophecy of the role that Peter was to play among the disciples. Next, he gave him power over Hell. This is not the Hell of fire and brimstone that the Church once preached. It is Sheol or Gehenna, the Hebrew place for the dead. One of the things expected of the Messiah was that he would not leave his followers to languish there. Lastly, he gave him the power to bind and loose, and this again is an echo from the Hebrew prophets and priests. To bind and loose, with them, implied the power to make rules or to suspend them: in other words, Jesus gave Peter the power to make the new faith of the new Church which he had, in that moment, founded.

From that day on Peter became the leader of the disciples, and much later, when the Gospels were written, his name always headed the rest.

Jesus knew that his end was fast approaching. It was time to warn his followers, so he told them that shortly he would suffer and be killed.

Now it would be thought that Peter, who had given up all to follow his Master, would take every word he said as what we now call Gospel truth. It was not so. Peter had a mind of his own, with a streak of stubbornness in it. He had acknowledged Jesus as the Messiah. As Peter saw it, a Messiah did not die without having done anything for the Jews. He was there to carry them to victory. If not, what was the purpose of his coming? He concluded that Jesus was wrong. He told him so, and said that he was sure that his Master would not die.

Peter's euphoria angered Jesus, and, indeed, for a man about to face the most agonizing of deaths, it must have been hard to bear. Angrily, Jesus said to Peter, "Get thee behind me, Sathanas," a sharp rebuke but less violent than it appears. By "Sathanas," Jesus merely meant "temptation"; he would not let Peter weaken his resolve: it is clear that he saw what was in Peter's mind. Knowing what a bitter disappointment was in store for the disciple, he prophesied that when the crisis came, Peter would deny him before the cock crew.

Peter was wrong. Jesus was seized and dragged off to the Pretorium, where his trial would take place. It was the ruin of Peter's hopes that he was the Messiah, but still Peter followed him. It was a dangerous thing to do, and pointless, for he could not help Jesus. Perhaps he thought that by some miracle, Jesus would escape. He waited by a fire in the chilly Jerusalem night, but nothing happened. Then, at that hour before morning when a man's spirits are at their lowest ebb, he was asked, more than once, if he was one of those who went about in Jesus's company. He denied it, hotly, even cursing and swearing when he was not believed. A cock crowed, and Peter, now utterly destroyed in his hopes and his self-respect, left the Pretorium, weeping bitterly.

In the sacristy of St. Peter's, where priests robe for Mass, there is a large golden model of a crowing cock.

Jesus was crucified. Peter went back to his fishing. Then Christ appeared to him as he was at work. Three times Jesus asked him if he believed and three times he replied that he did. Three times

Penitence of Peter for denying Christ three times before the cock crows; panel on the inner side of Holy Door (V. Consorti, 1949)

he was given the order to feed his sheep, and he obeyed to the end of his life.

When Pope John XXIII raised the Sacrament at the Papal altar in St. Peter's, there was the sound of solemn music played by musicians in the dome. At their feet, in a great frieze of mosaic, ran the words, "Thou art Peter and upon this rock I will build my church"; the church, that is, of which Angelo Roncalli, once a chaplain for the army, was now the master.

III

NERO

Peter traveled: he spread the good tidings wherever he found listeners. It is a great pity that nowadays, when we think of him on his journeys, we think of him preaching the Gospel as we know it and read it—the gentle admonitions of the Sermon on the Mount, the call to love one's fellows. It sometimes puzzles us that, with so mild a message, he so quickly did what his Master had commanded, and founded churches wherever he went.

But in fact he preached fire and thunder and the end of the world. He had heard Jesus say, unmistakably, that the history of mankind would come to an end in his, Peter's, own lifetime. He was certain that he had seen the resurrected Christ and he was sure he would see him again, coming in glory, to judge the good and the wicked. The good would be those who, like him, believed. The wicked would be all the rest. Meantime, all there was to do was to pray, gather for the sacramental meal, and wait for the end of everything.

This tremendous doctrine did not turn him into a hot-eyed fanatic. His character did not change, and it seems probable that Jesus knew that nothing would ever change it, and for that very reason he chose him to be the foundation-stone of the Church. In spite of the imminent end of the world, Peter still insisted on making up his own mind about things, and he was still willing to change it if he was convinced he should. Most of us think we have those gifts. Very few of us have.

When Peter knew Jesus, his Master had walked the earth as a Jew and preached his message to Jews in terms Jews would understand. Moreover, the Messiah was, above all things, a Jewish Messiah. It seemed logical to Peter that the new faith that he had set out to spread was meant for the Jews. Certainly, it was not meant to destroy the Jewish religion. But some of his companions thought otherwise, in particular Paul, a man who had never spoken to Jesus as Peter had done, but whose belief in Him was as deep as Peter's. The question arose as to whether a Jewish follower of Jesus could break the law and eat with those who were uncircumcised, and yet still be saved when the final catastrophe came. Peter thought not. Paul thought they could, and must. Their dispute runs through the Acts of the Apostles and, indeed, considerably enlivens the pages: sometimes the fight grows distinctly heated.

But we need not assume, as some have done, that they quarreled. Neither were small men: on the contrary, Paul is a towering figure in world history and Peter—obstinate, cautious, changeable, and unpredictable as he was—had also the gift of magnanimity. In the end he agreed, not without some backing and filling, with Paul. It was Peter who baptized the first Gentile, one Cornelius. Peter was a man who had once been wrong, and been forced to admit it. He had learned his lesson.

Both Peter and Paul found themselves in Rome, where they preached to the Jewish community there, and to others who would listen. It was inevitable that they should. Rome was the center of the known world and they went there as the founders of a new faith today would go to New York or Los Angeles.

Let us go back for a moment to St. Peter's. Let us stand where the Pope stood at the altar and think ourselves back to the days when Peter and Paul were alive.

There is no church. There is not even a temple. We are standing on the top of a hill called Vaticanus. It is covered in vineyards. The wine the grapes produce is notoriously bad. Down in the sprawling city below us it is said that the man who can drink Vatican wine can drink anything. As we look toward Rome, on our right are the walls of an arena built by the Emperor Caligula for chariot racing. Caligula is dead, cut down for the madman he had undoubtedly become. In his place, a handsome,

25

Nero to set going a rumor that it was these Christians who had set fire to Rome.

The rumor gained ground, and the Emperor, well pleased, ordered that Christians should be put to death as common criminals. In the Roman world, executions were often added to public entertainment as an attractive tidbit: an advertisement has been found in Pompeii which, after giving the list of gladiators, adds that several criminals will also be crucified, as a sideshow.

The executions took place in the circus that Caligula had built on the Vatican hill. Some Christians were wrapped in straw, covered in pitch, and set up on poles. The straw was then set on fire. These Christians were the lucky ones, for they would have been suffocated by the smoke before the flames reached their bodies. Others were torn to pieces by wild beasts; others were crucified. Among these last was Peter.

He was the leader of the Christian community and death by crucifixion was probably reserved for him because it was considered the most ignominious way to be put to death. So much shame was attached to crucifixion that the early Christians could not bring themselves to use the cross as a symbol of their faith: that came much later.

By custom, the body of a crucified person was given to his relations or friends. Peter was buried close by the circus, his corpse simply being put in a hole in the ground.

28

Relief of Peter crucified from Memorial of Sixtus IV outside the Chapel of St. Peter (Antonio Pollaiolo, fifteenth century)

Now it is the mark of a true Christian in any age that he wishes to approach as near as possible, by whatever means, to the founder, and this was poignantly so in the very earliest days. Peter had witnessed the tremendous events in Palestine. He had been specially chosen by Jesus to found a church, both when Jesus was alive and after he had risen. While Peter was living, to be with him was as close as the Christians could get to Jesus, until the second coming, which he so confidently predicted.

Peter had died on the cross, and the second coming of Christ did not take place. But Peter's bones lay on the Vatican hill and where they lay became the most revered spot in Rome for every Christian. The Christians in Rome were mostly poor people, often, but not always, under persecution. For two centuries they did not even build themselves a church, but merely met in one another's houses. It is probable that for years the Christians did not dare to mark the spot where Peter was buried, cautiously carrying its location in their memories.

But at the end of the second century, one Gaius wrote a letter in which he says that he has seen a "trophy" marking the grave on the hill. By "trophy" he meant a monument. It could not have been big or ostentatious. Christians were still liable to sporadic campaigns against them by the Emperors. Martyrdom was something to be expected as part of being a believer, though there were long periods in which the Christians were left in peace.

Whether they were at peace or being persecuted, the Christians grew in numbers. Then, in the fourth century, they were accepted into the State by the Emperor Constantine. His mother was a devout Christian and the first pilgrim to the Holy Land. But more importantly, Christians were some of Constantine's best soldiers.

Constantine was an extraordinary man. He wore a green wig. He was very interested in religion although nobody knew what his religion really was. He is said to have been baptized, but only in the last moments of his life. We do not know if he ever really believed in Christianity. He put his wife to death by locking her up in a steam bath and raising the heat until she was boiled alive. It is unlikely, then, that he was impressed by the teachings of the Sermon on the Mount.

OVERLEAF *Statue of Constantine, Scala Regia (Gian Lorenzo Bernini, 1670)*

IV

THE FIRST BASILICA

But it really did not matter whether Constantine believed in Christianity or not. The point was that he approved of Christians. Two and a half centuries had passed since the crucifixion and Christians had become thoroughly respectable. They no longer believed that the world would be destroyed in their own lifetimes. They believed that Christ would come in glory, because he had promised that he would, but they did not know when it would happen. Meantime, there was Heaven waiting for them when they died. To enter Heaven they knew they had to live honest and pure lives here on earth, doing good to their neighbors and harm to no man. Constantine, who was a shrewd man, saw that such people would make ideal civil servants, and with a vast empire to run, that was a class of persons he badly needed. He gave them positions in his court—that is to say, in the government—and they did very well. Christians, who had begun by being a nuisance to Rome, had now become pillars of society.

It was a society that badly needed shoring up. Romans had never been passionately attached to their own religion, and by Constantine's time they had ceased to believe in it at all. They had borrowed most of their gods from the Greeks, but they were not a very inspiring contingent. They were immoral, quarrelsome, and self-indulgent. It was difficult to worship them, and when certain Roman Emperors were officially declared by the Senate to be gods as well, it became preposterous. In Constantine's day, no intelligent man thought the gods really existed.

But, as often happens, the less the Romans believed in their gods, the bigger and more splendid were the temples they built to honor them. The Christians believed in their faith to the point of dying for it, but they had no temples at all. They had catacombs in which they buried their dead, but these were not used as places of worship except in the times of the persecutions. They simply continued to gather together in one another's houses as they had done in the earliest days: under the pavements of many Roman churches today, the ruins of those houses can still be seen.

When Constantine approved Christianity he saw that this had to be put right. The Christians would have to have temples as big and as splendid as those of the old gods, or else the other Romans would never take them seriously.

One of the first things that he did was to order that a huge building be raised over the tomb of Christ in Jerusalem. This structure was so vast it took in the hill that was traditionally believed to be Golgotha. Constantine shaved off the top of the hill to make it fit in with the architecture, with the result that today on the hill of the crucifixion is a singularly undistinguished chapel approched by a narrow flight of stairs.

But this was in Jerusalem, which was a long way from Rome. Constantine needed something nearer. He decided to build an even vaster temple over the tiny shrine that stood above the place where Christians held that St. Peter had been buried. His intentions are clear. He wished to build something so obviously expensive that the Romans would feel that if the Emperor could spend so much money on an obscure sect, there must be something in it. That is another reason why St. Peter's is the biggest church in the world today.

Let us see what Constantine put in place of the vineyards in which we walked.

The Vatican hill is no longer so steep. Constantine has leveled a lot of it, just as he had leveled the top of the hill of Golgotha. We go through massive doors into a vast courtyard. This is the atrium and the notion is taken from Roman villas of the time. The atrium was the place where the owner of the house met his

Niches in the wall of a tomb in the necropolis

RIGHT *Burial urns in arched nooks in the necropolis*

visitors and often transacted business. It is laid out as a garden with a fountain in the middle. It is so beautiful that Christians call it "Paradise."

If we are sinners, we can go no further. If we are in good standing with the clergy, we can go into the church.

Two rows of gigantic columns line an open space at the far end of which we can see a shrine. It gleams with precious marbles, and it is guarded by six columns, twisted like sticks of barley sugar. Inside all this is the simple trophy, or monument, that Gaius saw. If we explore further we find four other rows of columns, making two aisles on either side of the central space.

If we are Romans the whole design will be familiar to us. Constantine had simply taken over the plan of Rome law courts, putting St. Peter in the place where normally the judge would sit. These halls were called basilicas, and the choice of design was tactful. The only other indoor places where Romans congregated were the public baths, magnificent affairs which would have done very well for churches except for the fact that the Christians abhorred them as the centers of sexual vice of every description. As for temples, the pagan Romans rarely went inside them. Sacrifices were made on an altar outside the steps.

Thus St. Peter's today is called a basilica, but it is not. All of Constantine's church is gone, and St. Peter's today is built on a quite different plan. But he put up another basilica, this one in honor of St. Paul. This still stands, entirely rebuilt, but keeping

The Basilica of St. Paul (Bettmann Archive)

Constantine's design. St. Paul's-Without-the-Walls is a very good rendition of what the first St. Peter's must have looked like. It is awesomely big: it is austere. The first St. Peter's was much more solemn than the one we have now. It was built to honor St. Peter, not for the glorification of Popes. But then, at that time the Pope was a nobody who had suddenly become somebody on the nod of the Emperor—an Emperor who might easily change his mind about the whole business of Christianity, as his predecessors had done more than once.

This, then, was St. Peter's own church and tradition has it that Constantine treated his bones with reverent care. He gathered them into a box of wood on top of which (or perhaps, over it) he placed a massive gold cross. He did not change his mind about Christianity. Throughout his life he continued to send costly presents of gold and jewels to the shrine he had built, until it became the wonder and talk of the world.

The Roman Empire fell. The city was sacked again and again by barbarians, but it would seem that they left the shrine alone because they were Christians.

But the Saracens were not. On the contrary, they considered it a religious duty to desecrate Christian shrines, to say nothing of looting the treasures of the churches in which they found them. In A.D. 846 they sailed up the Tiber and devastated the tomb of

The altar in the Basilica of St. Paul (Bettmann Archive)

St. Peter. From that day onward, nothing more was heard of Constantine's gold cross, or of any other of his gifts.

The Saracens went and did not come back to Rome, though they fought the Christians elsewhere for centuries. The Dark Ages gave way to the Middle Ages. The Popes grew powerful and rich. They could make and break kings, although sometimes the kings retaliated by making and breaking the Popes. But all the time the prestige of St. Peter's Basilica increased, and it became the ambition of every devout Christian to make a pilgrimage to the Apostle's tomb. The church grew splendid once again; it was hung with magnificent tapestries and ablaze with costly lamps. Then disaster hit it.

V

THE INSULT

The thirteenth century was drawing to its close. Christianity had been in existence for over a thousand years; St. Peter's had never been more rich; the Papacy never as powerful. Things were going so well that the Pope declared that the year 1300 should be a Jubilee—a year of rejoicing and rededication. All who could were called to make a pilgrimage to Rome. All Europe responded. Rome, for a year, became the center of the world, as it had been before. It was said at the time that over two million people made the trip. That figure may be too large. What is certain is that so many people came that pilgrims were crushed to death as they crossed the bridge over the Tiber that led to St. Peter's. At the shrine itself, two priests stood by daily with rakes to haul in the offerings.

The Pope was Boniface VIII, and the right sort of man to stand at the peak of power—or so it seemed in the year of the Jubilee. We know what he looked like. We have no portrait of St. Peter: we have virtually none of his successors down to Boniface, save for some formal pictures in stiff mosaics. But centuries later, when St. John Lateran was being restored, a column was cleaned and there was found a lively and realistic picture of Boniface, painted by Giotto from the life. The Pope is on St. Peter's balcony, giving his benediction to pilgrims, exactly as the Pope is seen to-day in myriads of households. It is a fresco and it may claim to be the first newspicture in history.

Boniface has a heavy, determined face and piercing eyes. He is every inch a Pope and he is clearly a man with whom one would not readily argue. The chronicles of the time report that he had a terrible temper.

One man, however, stood up to him, and the result was a quarrel that changed the whole history of St. Peter's. This man was Philip, King of France. Philip had need of money, for he had another quarrel on his hands. England laid claim to a great deal of France, and war was inevitable. They were changing times. Both countries were slowly realizing themselves as nations, independent of distant Popes. Philip wanted his newly-born nation to keep back at least some of the torrent of gold that was pouring into Rome from French churches and monasteries. Philip maintained that the Pope could lay down the law in matters

44

Boniface VIII (Giotto) (Bettmann Archive)

of the faith, but outside of that, he could not. The two men did not mince words. Philip wrote to him, "To Boniface, who calls himself Pope, little or no greeting. Let your Stupendous Fatuity know that in temporal matters we are subject to no man." Boniface, the six-foot-tall priest who still stares out at us from the column in St. John Lateran, was at no loss for a reply in kind. "Our predecessors," he wrote back to Philip, "have deposed three kings of France. Know—we can depose you like a stable boy, if it prove necessary."

There was substance in the threat. Boniface could excommunicate Philip. The power of the Church was such that it could issue a command that the faithful need not pay the King their taxes, nor debtors pay him their debts. Whether the faithful would obey the Pope or the King's law-enforcement officers was a point that had not been decided. The idea of a sovereign state with a unique command over the loyalties of its subjects was very new.

If the Pope held the weapon of excommunication, Philip had one that was just as sharp, and that was a conspiracy. Boniface had a devoted enemy. To enrich one's own family was an accepted practice among the Popes of the times, but Boniface had done it with a ruthlessness that had no parallel. There was an immensely wealthy family called the Colonnas, and Boniface had used his supreme power to loot them without mercy. When they rebelled, he did not hesitate to destroy a whole city to teach them a lesson. The head of the family, Sciarra Colonna, fled from Rome to safety. It was Philip's opportunity. A French envoy was sent to Italy. He met Sciarra in secret, and together they drew up a plot against Boniface.

The Pope did not always stay in Rome. In some seasons its streets were too foul, its population too fond of brawling, to make it a comfortable place in which to live. Boniface often preferred to stay in the little hill town of Anagni, within easy reach of the city, but away from its squalors.

On September 6, three years after the triumphant Jubilee, a band of armed men broke into Anagni and made for the palace of the Pope. They were led by Sciarra Colonna, aided by an emissary of Philip.

They searched for the Pope with drawn swords. They found him. Knowing that he was going to be killed, Boniface had put on his Papal robes and the great tiara with its three jeweled crowns. He sat on his throne, and, immobile, awaited his death. The sight of this man, fearless and arrayed in all the majesty of his office, so enraged Sciarra that he bounded up the seven steps of the throne and raised his sword. He would have plunged it into the Pope, but his French fellow-conspirator stayed his hand.

Boniface was dragged off to prison, and for three days Sciarra Colonna kept him there while he and the Frenchman argued as to what was to be done to him. Then the citizens of Anagni, having recovered from the shock, turned on the conspirators and forced them to release the Pope, who, after all, was the mainstay of the town merchants. The conspirators barely escaped with their lives.

Boniface was free, but to no purpose. He returned to Rome, but he was half-mad with rage and chagrin. He locked himself away, sure that anyone who came near him meant to capture him. In a month he was dead, not from suicide as was thought by some, but from sheer shame.

His successor on the throne of St. Peter lasted only a year. Then Philip won. With the terrible-tempered Boniface out of the way, the French cardinals in the conclave managed to elect a French Pope, Clement V. Once the tiara was safely on his head, he packed up his bag and baggage (and the Papal treasure) and moved his whole court to France. He settled in Avignon, and stayed there, the tool of the French King.

The Papacy stayed in Avignon for seventy years. It was known to Catholic writers as the Babylonian Captivity.

VI

RUIN

For Rome, the Pope's departure was a catastrophe. The city had lived off the back of the Papacy: now, suddenly, there was no money at all. It all went to Avignon, as Philip had fully intended. The population of Rome rapidly sank into such abject poverty that thousands left. Rome, which at the time of Constantine had over a million citizens, had now a bare thirteen thousand. Grass grew in the deserted streets; buildings collapsed and were not repaired. People, such that there were, lived in hovels among the Imperial ruins.

But the most striking effect of all was upon St. Peter's. Without the Pope, the basilica died. The services at the tomb of the Apostle dwindled and then stopped completely. The innumerable lamps went out because there was no one to light them and no one to buy the oil. Cows wandered in from the countryside, which had already crept well within the walls of the city. They browsed in the atrium and one dismayed observer saw them even licking the altar in the basilica itself. St. Peter's had been a burial ground for Popes, cardinals, and saints. Wolves came in and dug up their bodies in the night.

Deserted and dark on the Vatican hill, St. Peter's began slowly to fall apart. The south wall tilted outward till it was six feet out of true, and the beams of the roof dragged the north wall with it till Constantine's great basilica was like a box askew.

Seventy years later the Popes came back. The Romans cheered the first to return in a wild delirium in Piazza Navona. He found he could not live in his palace, which was then the Lateran, because it was in such a state of ruin that it was beyond repair. He hastily knocked together some rooms on the Vatican hill, and moved there. The Popes have been there ever since.

The state of St. Peter's was not much better. Pope Nicholas V asked his architect what could be done about it and he was told that it should be torn down. An earthquake shock would bring the whole thing down on the Pope's head and those of his faithful. The Pope agreed. The building of a new church was put in hand. The church as we know it was born. Three hundred and thirty-seven years later it was finished.

CLEMENS·V·PP·VASCO·

Clement V (Bettmann Archive)

NICOLAVS·V·PAPA·SERGIANENSIS

Nicholas V (Bettmann Archive)

VII

THE BONES OF ST. PETER

The old basilica had been built to honor St. Peter's grave. The new one had the same purpose. But was St. Peter still there after all the trials the church had been put to? Had the Saracens scattered his bones? Had the wolves eaten them? These are questions that no one dared to answer right down to our own times. I shall now tell the strange story of the mortal relics of Simon called Peter; to do so I shall have to pass rapidly through the centuries and come down to an obstinate woman of our own times, who impressed one Pope, was snubbed by a second, convinced a third, only to be snubbed again. If his bones are in his church, then this woman is responsible for finding them, and she alone: if, I repeat, they *are* there.

Constantine, as we know, built a shrine around a shrine. But by the early Middle Ages, the first shrine had sunk out of sight. In A.D. 594 Pope Gregory the Great had raised the floor of the basilica, so that the tomb was now beneath the pavement. It could only be seen by going through a passage in the crypt. His reasons were sound. The tomb had accumulated a vast treasure of silver and gold plate and jewels. The times were troubled and it was safer out of sight. Besides, the approach through the crypt passage added mystery and awe to the pilgrim visit.

Another Pope put it a little further underground by building a new altar on top of the one Gregory had placed over the tomb. All this was kept intact in the new church, but Clement VIII raised a great new altar high over the other two. This is the one at which I saw John XXIII celebrate his coronation Mass.

Now in all this time, nobody of any importance had seen the buried shrine. It stands to reason that some common workman must have caught a glimpse, but it would have terrified him. Gregory the Great had laid what amounts to a curse on anyone who should disturb the Apostle. The Roman Empress (now in Constantinople) had written to him asking him for a relic, for which she drew down Gregory's thunder on her head. It would be, he said, "an intolerable and sacrilegious thing" to touch St. Peter's bones, and he told a horrifying tale of the disasters that had fallen on those who had so dared.

This curse was so effective that for more than a thousand years nobody else had the courage to challenge it. During this long time there were rumors that somebody had seen a tomb of mosaic with a body lying on a marble slab; someone else had seen a grave from which came a sweet perfume. But these were just tales. The tomb, with whatever it contained, lay unseen and undisturbed.

Then came the new St. Peter's. In the seventeenth century the reigning Pope decided to raise a great bronze canopy over the last of the altars that had been built over the sunken grave. The columns supporting the canopy would have to have foundations and this meant disturbing the holy earth around the Apostle. "Immediately," says the chronicler of these events, "everybody was talking about the warning of Gregory the Great." There was a strong feeling among the clergy that it should not be done. But the designer, Bernini, had the gift of getting his own way with the Pontiffs, and Clement VIII finally gave orders that the foundations should be laid, but with the great reverence. To make the occasion even more solemn, the work was begun on the day of Feast of St. Peter and St. Paul.

Ten days later the cleric in charge of the work fell dead. This was sensational enough, but more was to follow. He had dropped dead in the morning. The same afternoon his assistant died. A few days later there was another tragedy: the secretary to the first cleric also died. Panic now spread among the workmen, who now point-blank refused to continue the work. It would appear that some of the persons surrounding the Pope kept their heads and suspected foul play. Suspicion fell on the servant of the second dead man and he was condemned to be hanged.

This may or may not have been just, but it did nothing to dispel the terror and gloom that the affair had created. When the Pope himself fell sick, the people of Rome could stand the strain no longer. They demonstrated on the streets, as they regularly do to this day when their feelings are worked up to the boiling point.

Rome demonstrations are very sincere and very passionate. But they blow over. It was just so on this occasion. Bernini bided his time and did not offer to alter a jot of his plans. In due course he offered the workmen extra wages and the digging quietly began again. But the scare had been so great that nobody approached the Apostle's tomb. The foundations were laid: the tomb remained unseen.

This is how things remained until 1939. Pius XI had died. Pius XII succeeded him. The new Pope was a Roman aristocrat with a wide culture. His predecessor had asked to be buried as near to the tomb of St. Peter as possible, and while the grave was being dug archaeological fragments came to light which roused the new Pope's curiosity. He gave orders that the excavations should continue and finally, once more on the Feast of St. Peter and St. Paul, he boldly decided to do what no Pope had dared to do before him: he gave orders that the whole area of the tomb should be explored. It was a blow to millennia of superstition, and very much to his credit.

From the first Pius XII's courage and curiosity were rewarded. The excavators discovered that running under St. Peter's was a Roman cemetery. It looked a little like a street of houses. Families had put up square rooms with proper entrance doorways, some with columns. Inside these were niches in which the urns containing the bones or ashes were placed. Other cemeteries of this nature have been discovered all over the Roman world but this had a peculiarity. We have seen that Constantine shaved off the top of the hill of Golgotha. He had shaved off the top of this row of tomb-houses as well.

Now, the ancient Romans had a strong dislike of disturbing the dead. If Constantine had decided to destroy a cemetery, at least in part, he must have had a powerful reason for doing so. This could only have been that St. Peter's Basilica could have been built on that spot and no other. Clearly, then, he had built it over and around the Apostle's grave, which could not be far away.

The exploration continued. Then, one day, the excavators came upon the very shrine that Gaius had described. It was quite modest, no taller than a man, and it had a niche which pilgrims, in the Dark Ages, had described. It was, without doubt, the shrine that Constantine had enclosed, though his monument, with all its splendors, had largely disappeared.

The shrine was, in fact, a sorely battered ruin: the Saracens had done their work well. But at its foot was a square stone set into the ground at a curious angle to the monument. The archaeologists were immediately excited. It looked exactly as though the slab marked the grave that the monument had been put up to celebrate.

In an atmosphere of great tension, the slab was raised. There was, indeed, a grave underneath, but it was empty. It bore signs that at some time—it was impossible to say when—it had been disturbed. Some bones were discovered, but they were in the margin of the area of the monument, and, rather rashly, it was claimed at first that they were the remains of St. Peter. But the Pope was dubious. The bones were closely examined and it is now quite sure that they are not.

This is how things would have remained if it had not been for a remarkable woman. For learned skill, persistence, and brilliant intuition she is one of the most extraordinary women of her time, but nobody outside of Italy seems to have heard of her. Perhaps this is because she describes what she did in virtually unreadable books. She is one of those geniuses who should never be allowed to describe what they are doing in their own words.

Her name is Margherita Guarducci and she is a professor of ancient inscription in the University of Rome. Now, one of the big disappointments of the digging beneath St. Peter's was that no inscriptions of any sort had been found that could possibly refer to St. Peter or his grave. This was strange, since Romans were

ABOVE AND RIGHT *A tomb in the necropolis*

LEFT *Monument of Pius XII in the Chapel of St. Sebastian (Francesca Messina, 1964)*

extremely fond of writing things up on pieces of stone. Pontius
Pilate did it and that is the reason why we know that he really
existed. True, on a short side wall that had been built to one side
of the monument, the excavators had found an inextricable mass
of *graffiti*—letters scratched and scribbled on the wall by visitors.
They were so confused that the archaeologists could make nothing of them. There was certainly nothing about St. Peter that
could be disentangled.

Or so it seemed until Guarducci took a hand in the matter. She
saw a photograph of one scribble in which the letters were clear
but made no sense, since some of them were missing. The letters
were in Greek but I can perhaps show how they appeared to Guarducci by translating them into English, where the writing would
be something like this:

PET   S   RE

Guarducci took the first three letters to be the beginning of the
word Peter, for no better reason, I fancy, than that she rather
hoped they would be. Then, after prolonged study (and it was
far more difficult than I am making it seem), she decided that the
full careless scrawl read, in Greek:

PETER IS HERE

Her next step was to go to the excavation and see the actual
inscription. It had been taken away. Doggedly, she traced the
piece of plaster down and set about putting it back. To her aston-

ishment she found that close by was a sort of long box, partly lined with marble, and inserted into the wall. The box was clearly a tomb—a tomb in which someone had scrawled just before it was closed the message "Peter is here."

But there was nothing in the wall-tomb at all.

She set about deciphering the other inscriptions in the side wall and after years of work she definitely established that they were Christian symbols, presumably scratched by pilgrims. She searched the catacombs of Rome for similar ones, and she found them.

She next went to see Pope Pius XII. She was so excited by what she had to tell him that she could barely speak. Pope Pacelli, the most courteous of men, closed the door of the room in which they met so that the comings and goings that surround a Pope should not disturb her. Once alone, she poured out her story to the Pontiff. He was impressed by what he heard. He encouraged her to go on.

She now made an inspired guess: she made up her mind that something had been found in the tomb. She called for the diary of the excavations where every discovery would be recorded. The Pope had put the work into the hands of a worthy and industrious friend who was not, however, a trained archaeologist: to her utter dismay, she found that no diary had been kept.

Almost anybody else but Guarducci would have given up. She

did not. She got hold of one of the workmen who had been there when the tomb was discovered, and cross-questioned him. He was a sampietrino, one of the specialized masons who keep St. Peter's in repair. He remembered the finding of the tomb, and he remembered that something had certainly been in it, to wit, human bones.

Where were they now? The sampietrino was not at all sure, but together they searched the cellars of St. Peter's, and in one of the dampest of all, they found the bones. They had been put into a wooden crate, still wrapped in the purple cloth in which they had been found.

Guarducci had another interview with the Pope. But by now it was Pope John XXIII. He was fatherly: he was full of goodness and kindness toward her. But when she began talking about her book which she had published on the inscriptions, he began talking about *his* book which he had written on the life of St. Charles Borromeo. It is the surest way of silencing any author. Pope John was not interested in her theories and she left his presence depressed, but by no means defeated. She went on with her researches.

She had her troubles. She even, at times, had her doubts, like St.

Peter himself. The worst moments came when, attentively examining the bones, she saw that some of them looked as though they belonged to some small animal. This was a decided setback, and she may well have decided that it was fatal, particularly since she was receiving a barrage of criticism from other experts in her field.

So, at the same time, was the Papacy. John XXIII had gone, deeply loved and admired. He had "opened the windows," as he had said, and a new wind was sweeping through the Church. But the Ecumenical Council he had called had begun to question whether the successor of St. Peter should really have the absolute power over the faithful that he had always claimed. Paul VI came to St. Peter's Chair, and considered it his duty to stop the rocking of St. Peter's boat. Guarducci went to see him. He immediately showed an intense interest in anything to do with the first among the Apostles. He told her to go ahead with her researches, with his blessing.

She had the bones examined by doctors and anthropologists. Some were certainly those of a small animal: in fact, a field mouse. It was a crisis for Guarducci, and she bent all of her formidable energies to solving it. She asked archaeologists who had dug up bones in Ostia, Pompeii, and other places if they had come across the same thing. They had.

Then, in a brilliant flash of intuition, she saw the answer. Tradition had it that Peter was buried after his crucifixion in a grave scraped from the bare earth. What could be more natural than a mouse creeping into the holy spot and dying there?

She went back and studied the box-tomb. Exercising a brilliant archaeological skill, she established that the tomb had not been touched since Constantine's day. Her critics maintained that the material in which the bones were wrapped was not purple (an Imperial color, worn only by the very great) but red. She established that the Imperial color was, in fact, red. She did this by testing dye made from the very same shellfish that, as we know, the Imperial purple was made from.

Her theory was now complete. Constantine had built a marble shrine for St. Peter around his monument—something which inevitably attracted the attention of robbers. Either he, or the Christians in charge of the building, had removed the relics of St. Peter to a safer place. The place was still within the shrine, but it was to one side, in the box in the wall, where a thief in a hurry would not look: in a word, in the wall that carried the inscriptions of the earliest pilgrims.

She presented her findings to Paul VI, and then, as is the way of the Vatican, heard no more about the subject.

But on the morning of June 26, 1968, amidst a great gathering of the faithful, and in the basilica itself, the Pope announced that the authentic bones of St. Peter had been found.

It was the triumphant moment of Margherita Guarducci's life. Or it would have been. The trouble was that nobody had thought of asking her to the ceremony. Why? She does not know. But we may guess. Guarducci was, after all, a woman, and the Vatican is always the Vatican.

The bones, which she alone had identified, were enclosed in plastic containers and replaced in the tomb-box which she alone had proved to be the true grave of the Apostle. It was a modest ceremony, with only a few Vatican officials present and a notary to record the event. But at least this time Guarducci was there, down in the bowels of St. Peter's, where she had spent years of her life.

The Pope has declared that the bones of St. Peter do really lie under the Papal altar. The Pope is infallible (according to current Catholic teaching), but only when he speaks *ex cathedra*, that is, from the Chair of St. Peter, or, as we have seen, from underneath it. This the Pope did not do. The Pope—and Guarducci—could be wrong. What is the truth?

When it is proposed to make a person a saint, the Vatican has an interesting custom. It appoints a clever cleric to oppose all the evidence that the person in question was holy and to bring out proof that he or she was not. He is called the Devil's Advocate. Let me assume that role about Peter's bones. There are questions to be asked.

The first question is whether we have any real evidence that St.

The bones of Peter in the niche of the original shrine, where they were discovered by Margherita Guarducci

Peter ever came to Rome. In the first Epistle of St. Peter, he says he is writing from Babylon. Rome was often called Babylon among Christians and Jews because it was so corrupt, so this is promising. But did St. Peter write the Epistle? It is largely concerned with warning the various new churches to gird themselves to face a terrible persecution. But in St. Peter's lifetime there was no persecution of the Christians at all, except the one in which he is believed by tradition to have lost his life. Does it not seem more probable, then, that the Epistle was written in his name much later, when terror was indeed threatening the new faith?

Next, how can it be believed that Constantine, who lavished untold fortunes in building churches, who erected an expensive monument over the tomb, who, throughout his life, continued to embellish it with costly presents, would tuck the holy relics away in a wall-tomb which was not even completely lined with marble? One would expect him to line it with gold plate. In fact, the top was left without any decoration at all.

Let us suppose, nevertheless, that that is what he did. How can we be sure that the bones that Guarducci found in the damp cellar were really the ones that were found when the tomb-box was first discovered? No record was kept of the progress of the excavations. No identifying slip was found in the wooden chest to which the bones were removed.

The excavations were all very unscientific, and in our age it is unwise to ignore science, an observation that leads me, as the

67

Devil's Advocate, to my concluding question: why were the bones not submitted to a radiocarbon test, which would have dated them, without the possibility of a doubt, to within one hundred and fifty years of their true age?

The Devil's Advocate rests his case. Now, for the summing up.

Guarducci has produced a great deal of proof that the bones are St. Peter's and nobody has shown that they are not. As she herself has said, a great number of archaeological discoveries have been accepted with far less evidence. I have myself stood on a hill and seen the walls of Jericho, and I have seen that the oldest wall of all did actually fall down. Does one need someone to dig up the trumpet to believe that the Bible story has at least some touch of history in it?

There are some things we can never know for sure. It is *probable* that St. Peter came to Rome. It is *probable* that he died in the first persecution of the Christians. It is now quite certain that the great basilica shelters the remains of what the early followers devoutly and passionately held to be the monument erected over his tomb. That fact, alone, is a lot.

VIII

ST. PETER'S AS A
WORK OF ART

I have described the old St. Peter's as a historical monument.
I have shown why it was built and why it was built where it was.
But the new St. Peter's is something more.   It is a deliberate work
of art, and as such I shall, from now on, approach it.

The approach is not easy.   The Taj Mahal is also a deliberate
work of art.   But the Taj was built during the lifetime of one man.
St. Peter's took three centuries.   The beauty of the Taj can be
realized in fifteen minutes: that of St. Peter's takes many hours and
many visits, and the reason for that is money.

As Pope Paul VI has pointed out, the Catholic Church is not
nearly as rich as people think it is.   When it was decided to pull
down the tottering basilica of Constantine and build a new one,
there was not enough money in the Pope's purse to do it.   To get

around this difficulty, the Popes sold indulgences to the faithful. Indulgences have got a bad name, largely because people do not know what they really were. They were not a ticket-of-leave-to-sin. They were not even pardons. They were a means by which a believer could shorten the punishment of some dead person who was in Purgatory, or shorten his own if that was in store for him. Indulgences were quite logical. If St. Peter had been given the right to bind and loose, then his successors in the Church had the same power.

For a while the sale of indulgences was brisk, but Martin Luther and the Reformation slowed down the traffic to a trickle. From then on, time and again, the money for building St. Peter's ran out and work had to stop.

But one of the difficulties of being a Pope is that while you are alive you are one of the most famous men on earth, yet you are very much aware that when you are dead you have a very good chance of being completely forgotten. This is especially so if you are a good Pope and run the Church smoothly and quietly, as it should be run. Popes, therefore, are generally anxious to leave something behind them that will keep their name alive. One way of doing this was to push on with St. Peter's, and leave an inscription that said what had been done and at whose orders.

Some Popes have been extremely adept at this. Paul V for instance, built the façade. He put up a huge inscription right across the front, so that today it appears he built the whole church.

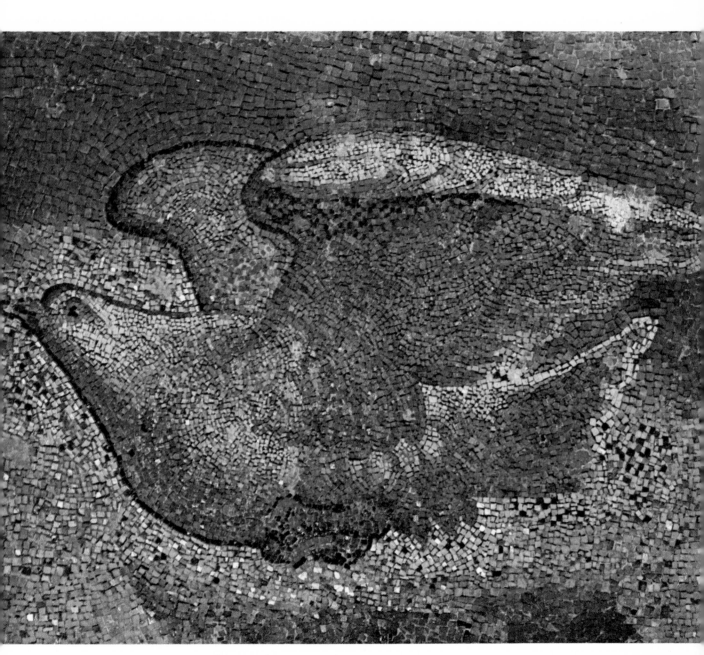

Mosaic dove in the Crypt of St. Peter's

Pius XII did not do very much. But he cleverly regilded the apse and had an inscription put on the work. Thus in every Papal ceremony his name blazes in great gold letters over the head of his successor, dominating the whole affair.

Two Papal inscriptions are most interesting, and anybody who wishes to study St. Peter's from the artistic point of view should begin his visit by studying them closely.

The first inscription is just inside the atrium, or porch, of St. Peter's, in front of the central door. It is a huge inlay of marbles on the floor. The principal features of the design are John XXIII's name, in letters that are surprisingly large for so modest a man, and the lion of St. Mark, which was his symbol. The other is similar, but much smaller. It is to be found on the floor in front of the chapel that holds Michelangelo's "Pietà." The chapel was restored by Paul VI, and this inlay carries his name.

Now St. Peter's is filled with the most exquisitely cut marble work to be found anywhere. It is also famed for a mosaic work-shop so accurate that the pictures over the altars, which look like oil paintings, are really mosaics. Yet Pope John's lion is a naive animal that looks like a startled cat, crudely cut, and stuck about with random bits of colored marble, as though a child had taken a hand in making it. It is the same with Paul VI's contribution. The inscriptions in St. Peter's are models of harmonious and justly proportioned letters. Yet this inscription sprawls and tilts clumsily across the floor, as though the mason could do no better. The letters are a faithful copy of the inscriptions of the late Roman Empire when, indeed, the masons had lost their skills.

Why? The reason is that they are in the artistic taste of our time, which is for the crude and unfinished and the primitive. The Popes who built St. Peter's employed the most famous artists of the day. The artists were famous because they followed, or sometimes set, the taste of the times. It is an excellent principle, and it has turned St. Peter's into a fascinating study for anyone who has not too prejudiced an eye. The basilica is not full of masterpieces: but it is the work of men who were masters. It is a gallery of what people thought was ideal beauty down through three hundred years. It is also a lesson. One can stand in front of the more insipid and feeble sculptures (as they seem to us) and wonder what, in three centuries' time, people will make of Pope John's childish lion.

The Popes, then, follow the tastes of the times: and they also know that the best chance they have of being remembered is to commission some work of art and put their name on it. Remembering those two things will make it easier to see what happened to St. Peter's, and why.

IX

BRAMANTE

Despite the fact that Constantine's church was falling down, and a new church had been decided upon, nothing much was done about it for many years after the Popes came back from Avignon. The Popes were largely too busy with the Papacy, which was in a state of almost comic confusion. At one time there were no less than three Popes, all wearing the tiara at the same time. The newly arising nations took their pick among them; England, for instance, backed one Pope and France, naturally, backed one of his rivals.

But things slowly straightened out, until there was once more only one Pope. During the squabbling, the old St. Peter's slowly continued to crumble. It was patched up and shored up, and a new choir was built, but no Pope was willing to undertake the task of wholly rebuilding, until, in 1503, Julius II came to St. Peter's Chair.

He was a Della Rovere, a plebian family which had exceedingly rough manners even for those times. One of Julius's brothers had killed one man before he was seventeen, and stabbed another to death when he was twenty-one. Julius fully shared in the family violence. He once told a sculptor to put a sword in his hand and not a book because he knew nothing about books but a great deal about fighting. Indeed, he drowned Italy in blood during his pontificate by unnecessarily making war. He was, however, far from being a mere military gorilla. He was a man of very keen intelligence who, in spite of a violent temper, had also a sense of humor. He was aware that a fighting Pope was something of an anomaly but he summed up the situation (and his own character) very neatly. "If we are not ourselves pious," he said, "why should we prevent other people from being so?"

In spite of his winning wars, he knew that, like his predecessors, he would be easily forgotten: since he never read books, he probably knew practically nothing about the Popes who had reigned before him, except through anecdotes. He therefore decided to commission works of art from the best-known artists. One of these was Michelangelo. Julius wanted him to carve the biggest tomb St. Peter's had ever seen. It was to be in the form of a pyramid on which would stand forty huge marble statues. Then he changed his mind and, as all the world knows, he set

77

OVERLEAF: RIGHT AND LEFT *Statue of Moses from the Tomb of Julius II (Michelangelo, 1516)*

Michelangelo to painting the roof of the Sistine Chapel instead.

But that idea was not grandiose enough for him. He made up his mind to do something striking and splendid about St. Peter's. He called in the most praised architect of the time, Bramante. Bramante, who knew the sort of man he was dealing with, told him that the most striking thing he could do would be to pull down St. Peter's and build the biggest and most awe-inspiring church history had ever seen. He produced a design. Julius, of course, was enchanted. In 1506, he laid the foundation stone himself. It was set in a deep hole into which, in his soldierly way, he boldly descended. The ceremony was somewhat hurried because Julius noticed that the hole was threatening to cave in. So, also like a good soldier, he beat a retreat and scrambled up again. But the new St. Peter's was begun.

In the history of St. Peter's, Michelangelo overshadows Bramante, which is a pity. Bramante was as good an artist as Michelangelo (who said he was) and he had as marked a personality, though it was less theatrical. He was born in Urbino and spent most of his life in the provinces, especially in Milan where he practiced as an architect. Then, when he was fifty-five, he decided to come to Rome to study the ruins, a remarkably humble thing to do, for middle-aged architects are usually convinced that they know all about their profession that there is to know.

He had very little money, but by planning a frugal way of life, he was able to go around Rome and painstakingly measure all the monuments that he could. The more he measured, the more profound was his admiration for the Roman architects. He determined to build like them.

He received some commissions in Rome and immediately impressed everyone with the cool, classic perfection of his work. By a strange coincidence he was engaged to build a shrine over the spot where it was mistakenly held that St. Peter was crucified. It was not on the Vatican hill but on the Janiculum. Bramante built a small temple so perfectly proportioned that it immediately became the model for taste. A year later Julius II asked him to work on St. Peter's.

He designed the church in the taste of the times, which he had done so much to set. But his work among the vast structures of the Romans had set his imagination on fire. He drew up a plan for a building as bold as the mightiest monuments of the past. In the plan a great open space was left around the tomb of the Apostle. Over this a gigantic dome was to be raised, based on that which covered Hadrian's Pantheon, which had survived intact. Four transepts were to radiate from this, all equal, in the form of a Greek cross. A great columned portico with two bell-towers completed the stupendous project.

His basilica was never built. Although every architect who followed him praised the design to the skies, not one of them (as is the way with architects) hesitated to alter it, including Michelangelo.

But the ghost of Bramante's church haunts the basilica. He got no further than putting up the four great piers that support the dome to this day. They are so enormous that a small church could be fitted into them. In fact, the church of San Carlo alle Quattro Fontane in Rome was built, by one of the architect's quirks, to cover exactly the same ground as the plan of the piers. Bramante had set the scale of the church: from then on, no man could make it mean.

He was a mild, cheerful man, obliging to the Pope and generous to his friends. He had none of the gloomy *terribilità* of Michelangelo, of whom one Pope said, "There is no dealing with the man." For all that, he thought as big.

Talented, generous, studious, and cultured, Bramante, then, appears to us to be a most agreeable man. It is all the more surprising to learn that he was the biggest vandal in the history of St. Peter's. The Saracens had merely devastated the tomb of St. Peter: Bramante laid the whole basilica waste.

Bramante advised Julius II to tear down Constantine's church and this may have been sound counsel; the walls, as we have seen, were perilous. But in the eleven centuries that had passed since its foundation, the basilica had become crowded with monuments, tombs, chapels and mosaics. Bramante tore these down, too.

The people of Rome watched the wholesale destruction with horror and dismay. As was (and is) their custom, they summed up their feelings by giving Bramante a nickname. They called him The Wrecker and warned Julius that if he continued to allow this sacrilege, something dreadful would happen to him.

Bramante defended himself by saying that the monuments made in the Middle Ages were uncouth, ill-made, and ugly. They would not do at all in the beautiful modern edifice, with its contemporary lines, that he and Julius meant to put up. Since all he left of the tombs of this period were a few fragments which he bundled away in the crypt, his argument may seem to have some substance. The fragments are not very impressive.

But as luck would have it for Bramante, one tomb escaped his hammer, and if we take the trouble to search it out, we can examine it and judge Bramante for ourselves. It is not in St. Peter's. It was moved to an obscure convent church in Rome; a place that is rarely visited even by the most thorough sightseer. It lies in the corner of the church of St. Balbina. It was made (and signed) by Giovanni di Cosma, one of the leading artists of his time. The sarcophagus is covered with a Gothic tracery of exquisite proportions. On top of it lies the figure of Cardinal Surdi. His face, carved with a chisel that seems as though it flitted across the stone, is profoundly human. It is so full of character that one feels one knows him: a gentle, soft man, full of kindness toward his fellow men, but, all in all, a little disillusioned with them. The statue has been carved with a chisel that seems as though it flitted across the stone. In a word, the tomb is a masterpiece. One stands in front of it and wonders how many more such beautiful things fell victim to Bramante's taste in art.

There was one monument that he dared not destroy. Had he done so the people of Rome would have lynched him. This was the great bronze statue of St. Peter, seated on a throne, and raising his hand in benediction. One foot is thrust forward: it has been worn smooth by the kisses of pilgrims. It was made by Arnolfo di Cambio in the thirteenth century. It is worth studying, for it gives us the key to Bramante's extraordinary behavior.

The robes, the hand, and the hair are well done. The face is serene, but somehow misses having the impact it should on us. Above all, there is a stiffness about the pose which at first seems to lend majesty to the figure, but after a while leaves the spectator with a feeling that the sculptor had not quite known how to pull off the statue that he had in mind.

This was exactly the feeling that Bramante and his fellow artists had about the artists of the Middle Ages, by and large. They thought them inept. They were overwhelmed by the realism of the ancient Roman statues that were continuously being unearthed, often by the Renaissance artists themselves. They strove to copy them: they hoped to learn how to sculpt as well, and even better. The only way to do better was to go back to Nature, as the Romans had done, and to study it. They studied Nature with a devoted passion, even going to medical schools to study corpses as they lay on the dissecting table. Leonardo da Vinci even drew careful studies of a hanged man.

The artists of the Middle Ages also studied Nature, but in the shape of birds and beasts and flowers which they carved, often with exquisite realism, in the nooks and crannies of their vast cathedrals. But they were shy of the human body. For them, a man or a woman was something to be seen through a veil of mysticism, a part of the whole drama of salvation through faith and prayer.

We can see that today. Bramante could not. We know so much more history than he did. We would not tear down an ancient monument to put up a new one. We preserve them with care. Still, in the matter of destruction we do pretty well, from time to time, with our bombs. In the twentieth century we do not mind destroying works of art, so long as we kill someone while we are doing it.

8 5

OVERLEAF *Bronze statue of Peter (attributed to Arnolfo de Camio, thirteenth century)*

X

MICHELANGELO

Bramante died, leaving a wrecked church behind him and two great piers which had been put up in such a hurry that they began to show cracks. Julius II died too, and a new Pope was elected. He was a Medici from Florence and he took the name of Leo X. His coronation was a very grand ceremony, but since there was no St. Peter's it took place in a tent put up just in front of the ruins of the church. There was not enough room in the tent for the guests, who sat crammed cheek to jowl. But it helps to understand St. Peter's if we reflect that Leo could have had himself crowned in St. John Lateran, or St. Paul's-Without-the-Walls, where there would have been room for everybody. But that was unthinkable. The successor of St. Peter had to be crowned hard by the Apostle's tomb, even if it had to be done under canvas.

The procession through Rome that followed made up for all the inconveniences. It was so magnificent that one contemporary observer wrote, very humanly, that he was seized by a very strong desire to be Pope himself. Classical Rome had, by this time, become a raging fashion. The Pope followed the fashion, as we have seen is the way of Popes. The procession was more pagan than Christian. Triumphal arches spanned the road, and nude boys, gilded all over, lent a touch which might well have been approved of by that same Nero who had started everything. Julius had left behind him a substantial treasure, part of which was to have been spent in rebuilding St. Peter's. One seventh of that money was spent by Leo on this single procession.

Very soon the rest of that treasure went. Leo had once said, "Let us enjoy the Papacy, since God has given it to us," and he threw himself into a round of banquets, dances, bullfights, and general entertainments, all on the scale of his coronation ride. He added great hunting parties to his amusements, to which he would invite one hundred and fifty guests. He hunted in boots and spurs and one querulous critic asked how anybody could kiss the Pope's toe if it was in a leather boot. The question might reasonably bother theologians, but it did not bother Leo at all. He continued to hunt and enjoy the Papacy. When he died the Vatican was bankrupt.

It may be imagined that, meantime, little was done about St.

Peter's. Architects were appointed, but since they built practically nothing, their names need not detain us. They built nothing because, of course, there was no money left over from the junketings. But Leo, like all other Popes, wanted to leave something behind him in stone and was anxious to get on with the new basilica. To raise the money, he took up the idea of indulgences, and decreed that a special issue of them should be made. By a happy chance, printing from movable type had recently been invented, so a mass-production of indulgences became possible. Leo brought Martin Luther down on the heads of his successors, and his idea for financing St. Peter's split Christendom. But he was not wholly bad. When he found that his agent, one Wrexel, was creating a scandal by his methods of promoting sales, he rebuked and dismissed him.

In any case, indulgences did not sell all that well. In fact, the Popes have never had enough money to build St. Peter's as it was meant to be built: there is a curious monument to the fact. The giant pilasters that decorate the interior look as though they are made of stone. They are made of stucco, which is much cheaper. Only the ones at the far end near the Chair of St. Peter are of marble, and some of these were put up in our own times.

It is difficult to write about the Papacy without giving the impression that the Popes were a scandalous lot. But that is because the bad Popes are more interesting (to a writer) than the good ones.

so he said) to have any meaning for him. All that concerned him was the salvation of his soul. The Pope was his spiritual master, and he was being asked to do something that was plainly a Christian duty. He grumbled to all his friends, but he did it. So profound were his feelings that he refused to take any fee.

It is something of a relief to learn that as soon as he got to work, he was back in his old form. He began with a blazing row. A competent but somewhat banal architect, Antonio Sangallo, had made a design for the basilica. It was a mass of columns and nooks, crowned with a dome that resembled a wedding cake. We know what it would have looked like because Sangallo made a huge wooden model of it. It took seven years to build and cost as much as a large parish church. It has survived to this day. It is kept in a room *inside* one of Bramante's piers, a good indication of the scale on which Bramante had built. Sangallo died before anything was done in the way of building. But he had staffed the Vatican with a large number of his relatives and friends, all of whom were making money out of the Papacy.

Michelangelo first dismissed the model as dull and impractical. It was full of places, he said, where thieves and prostitutes could hide at night and it would be impossible for the sacristans to winkle them out at closing time each evening. Having damned Sangallo's work, he next turned on Sangallo's friends and relatives, whom he accused of dishonestly taking money. They replied that Michelangelo had done exactly the same thing: he had been paid

Wood model of the basilica (Antonio de Sangallo, fifteenth century)

to do Julius's tomb, which he had never completed. This was scarcely Michelangelo's fault but it added useful fuel to the quarrel, which Michelangelo kept up to the end. If saving his soul meant forgiving his enemies, he was willing to face Purgatory rather than do it. Turmoil was essential to his genius, and in St. Peter's we see his genius in full flower.

When I was a boy of twelve and being exposed to works of art, I was taken to see the tombs of the Medici in Florence. Everybody knows the four reclining figures that Michelangelo sculpted for them, and which have been named subsequently Night, Day, Dawn, and Dusk. I was very impressed, but I said that they made me feel uncomfortable. I felt that they were going to slide off their curving bases at any moment. I was told not to be bumptious.

The person who would have been delighted to hear my remark was Michelangelo himself. That discomfort and tension that I felt was precisely the effect he aimed to produce in the spectator. The works of his youth have repose. The works of his later years struggle in the midst of a perpetual conflict of forces. Nothing is at rest, nothing is contained, except, marvelously, the whole. It is a style that is a reflection of the artist's own unquiet, but gigantic, personality.

Michelangelo's style reached its climax in his design for the apse of St. Peter's. Unfortunately, the apse is out of bounds to the general public, and it is the greatest of pities that it cannot easily be seen. Some time ago I spent two months inside the Vatican State; each day I would walk through the gardens, in which the apse was built. Each day I was overwhelmed with what I saw. The huge walls towered above me, but they were not cliff-like. They were alive and, after long inspecting, seemed to throb. Huge pilasters soared upward to struggle against a thick architrave which in turn was weighed down by a ponderous attic. The pilasters crowded windows, as though squeezing them, while the windows fought to escape. A profusion of pediments and cornices led the eye restlessly from point to point of the tremendous design, casting dramatic shadows in the strong Roman sun. Michelangelo had turned the apse into an enormous sculpture.

The apse was all Michelangelo built of the body of the church. His design was partially followed by other architects, but they were timorous. They softened the conflicts. They made everything more bland and more normal. Perhaps they were right. The greatest church in Christendom should not, perhaps, be the expression of one man's troubled soul.

We now come to the dome and one of the biggest ironies in the history of art. The dome is certainly the most beautiful ever erected. It is almost invariably described as Michelangelo's crowning masterpiece, the final proof of his transcendent genius. It might have been, if Michelangelo had designed it, but he did not. He built the drum: but even that is not as he wanted it. Each pair of the twin columns was to have a great statue above it, but these have never been put up. The drum finished, Michelangelo died.

To the day of his death, Michelangelo could not make up his mind about the shape of the dome. But we have evidence of the way his thoughts were running. One project of his has come down to us. It shows a huge, inverted bowl, almost a perfect hemisphere. It would not have soared gracefully as the dome does today. It would have weighed down on the church, immensely solid, giving an impression of power and not lightness. The dome today floats over Rome: the dome that Michelangelo wanted would have lowered over the city, a somber and perhaps a frightening monument, in tune with the last, anguished days of the master.

It is tempting to imagine the old man's rage if he could hear us praising him to the skies for something he never did, and probably would have detested.

The cost of the building of St. Peter's (and the way the money was raised) was one of the chief causes of the rise of Martin Luther. The Protestants had won great triumphs: whole populations had

Wood model of the basilica (Michelangelo, 1561)

left the Catholic Church. But the Protestants had not shaken the Papacy.

Pope Paul III had called a Council to reform the Church, but it was a very different one from the Council that was called in our own times. When Vatican II was over, it left the Papacy embattled. When the Council of Trent was done, the Popes were stronger than ever. Just because the Protestants cried "No Papacy," the Council of Trent, willy-nilly, made the Popes supreme and their absolute power beyond doubt.

A new confidence spread through Rome. It was a more sober place and more religious: that much the Protestants had done. Popes no longer set out to enjoy the Papacy that God had given them. Fortunes were no longer spent in banquets and processions: but they were spent in the building of new churches—large ones which were packed by the faithful. Rome was beautified in a hundred ways, not for the sake of town-planning or even art, but to show the triumphs of the Catholic faith over its enemies in a way that the man in the street—the great new streets that were cut through the old squalor—could not miss. Pope Sixtus V gave orders that all this should be crowned with the dome of St. Peter's.

Taste was changing, too. In the beginning of the Renaissance, men had been struck with awe at the achievements of the Greeks and Romans. As each new statue was unearthed, or each new ruin measured, all that artists and architects strove to do was to create as well. But as the decades wore on, they began to see that they were, in fact, equal to the ancients. Michelangelo, it was said, was even better. When they restored arms and legs and torsos to the mutilated statues of the ancients, they carved just as well, as we can see in any great museum today. When the group of the Laocoön was dug up, Michelangelo did not hesitate to carve a missing arm and fix it in the position he thought it should go.

With confidence came a lighter touch, in buildings, sculpture, and paintings. After a period in which everybody tried to imitate Michelangelo, without a touch of his genius, a new freedom began to be felt. The rules of the ancients were admired, but broken if fancy dictated something fresh. While the Protestants stripped their churches of all that could distract from the worship of God, the Catholics filled theirs with marbles where every gesture proclaimed the victory of the refound faith. The confidence of the Roman priests spread to Rome's artists.

The Pope chose Giacomo della Porta to carry on the work at St. Peter's, and he was instructed to put up the dome as quickly as it could be done. The original intention was, of course, to build the dome as the revered Michelangelo had designed it. But it did not please Giacomo della Porta. It would have been rash of him to say so, so great was the dead man's prestige. He took refuge in technicalities. He was not sure, he told the Pope, that

OVERLEAF LEFT *The cupola drum and stucco ceiling*

OVERLEAF RIGHT *The Cappella Clementini in the Chapel of St. Peter (Della Porta, 1600)*

he repeated the incident on a grander scale. He had been commissioned by Pope Innocent X to do the great Fountain of the Four Rivers in Piazza Navona, which has four giant figures and innumerable vents for the water. The Pope came to its inauguration. The basin and the vents were dry. Bernini, desolate, told the Pope that something had gone wrong with the water supply and there would be none that day. The Pope was very angry and began to stalk away. Bernini gave a signal. The Pope heard the sound of water. He turned back to find it pouring out of the fountain in great cascades. Innocent X was not a man with a sense of humor, but he, too, was greatly impressed by the *coup de théâtre*.

Bernini was, in fact, a man of the theater as well as a sculptor. He designed sets for the elaborate masques that were then much in fashion. They were very striking, according to all accounts. The audience demanded marvels, and Bernini supplied them. Angels flew among scudding clouds, volcanoes erupted, seas heaved, and gods and goddesses descended from heaven in flowery chariots. The stage apparatus for all this (concealed in beautiful buildings made of plaster) was known as the *macchina*, or machine. The word *macchina* was applied to all setups with a powerful theatrical effect.

And that gives us the key to St. Peter's. The great bronze baldachino, or canopy, which was designed by Bernini to cover the altar of the Apostle, was known to the workmen who put it up, and to

The baldachino covering the altar of the Apostle Peter (Gian Lorenzo Bernini, 1633)

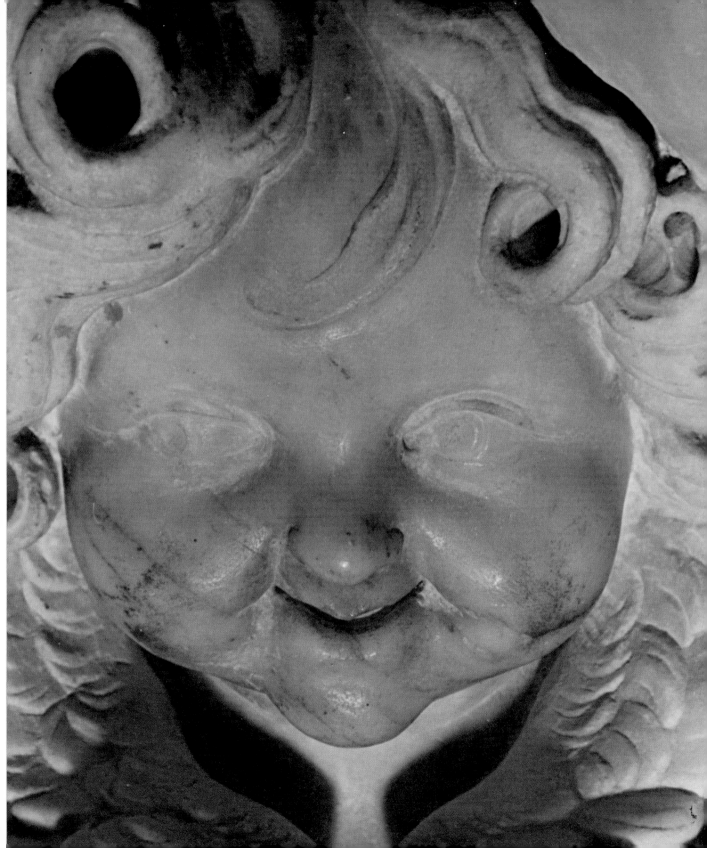

geously encased. The whole monument speaks as clearly as a poster and it can fairly be described as the most beautiful advertisement ever made. It has its subtle points, too. The Latin Doctors wear mitres, the Greeks are uncovered, a sign that the Greeks, like these two famous saints, should obey the Latins, which, in practice, they have always refused to do. Over all flies the dove of the Holy Ghost, depicted in a stained-glass window through which the sun shines with a striking effect. Even when it does not, there is a multitude of golden rays in stucco that imitates it. On great occasions the Pope (as we have seen) sits beneath this colossal composition on his throne. The Doctors dwarf him as a man, but they magnify him as a Pope.

Bernini had now set his mark on the far end of St. Peter's and in the middle. It was logical that he should decorate the new nave. Something had already been done: marble slabs to cover the columns had been begun, but the result threatened to look like the Pauline Chapel in Santa Maria Maggiore. By that time Bernini had trained a team of assistants who, without Bernini to overshadow them, would have been great artists in their own right. He set them to carving marble reliefs of the first thirty-eight Popes, each medallion to be supported by children, the whole to be sealed, as it were, with a dove, the symbol of the Pope who was paying the considerable bill. This gigantic task was completed in a year.

St. Peter's was now Bernini's. From the entrance door to the far end, his work prevailed. First came an admonition to doubters (such as Protestants). These thirty-eight men, said the great medallions, founded the Christian Church, often in their own blood. The Papacy was no Johnny-come-lately, like Martin Luther. Then the baldachino, soaring higher than a six-story Roman palazzo, a bronze fanfare proclaiming that in this place lay the first Pope of all, and on this Rock Jesus had founded his Church. Then on to the Chair, the Doctors, and the Holy Ghost, an ending to the story that announced that the story was going on and had no ending at all. Bernini had made St. Peter's, which seemed as though it would never be a whole, into one of the most unified churches ever built. Walking through it, I often think it a pity that the Popes had not waited for this wonder-child to be born, and let him put up the dome.

Alexander VII did the next best thing. He handed the piazza outside to Bernini, asking him to put it in order. For all his exuberance, Bernini was steeped in the ancients. We have seen how he chose the design of Constantine's columns for the baldachino. For the piazza he went even deeper into the past. Ancient Rome had been full of porticos, long, covered spaces held up by columns in which people could walk and talk all the year round, cool in the hot summer, sheltered in the mild Roman winter. He settled on this, but with a freedom that it is hard to find among the ancients, he bent these straight porticos into two grand semi-circles. Nothing like the piazza of St. Peter's had ever been seen before and nothing so successful has ever been built since. He himself said that he wanted to show how the church stretched out its protecting arms to the faithful to take care of them, and to the nonbelievers to convert them. He also made a drawing that showed the dome as God and the colonnade as His arms: but such conceits were merely the fashion of the time. To us, less fond of symbols, he had solved a practical problem in a practical way and made a stupendous work of art at the same time.

Bernini was a strange mixture, and, like most Neapolitans, a man of moods. When the occasion called for it, he could dress in the finest clothes and put on the finest manners. When Queen Christina of Sweden came to Rome, the Pope chose this sculptor to greet her at the gate of the city, out of all the courtiers and blue bloods he had at his disposal. Yet when Bernini worked he dressed in the coarse, sweaty gown of a stonemason: nor would he change it, whoever came to his studio. Popes came to chat with him. Queen Christina came. He still wore his stonemason's coarse dress. Queen Christina humbly kissed it.

He was no quarreler, like Michelangelo. He knew how to flatter Pontiffs in the Vatican. But in his studio he could be a terror, driving his assistants without mercy. He did not need to drive himself.   As he said, nothing interested him but his work.   In that, he was a towering egotist.   He would tolerate no rivals.   There was one sculptor who showed signs of a genius like his.   He was called Francesco Mochi, and Bernini so hounded him that he died early, a broken man.

As for Bernini, his fame grew so great that Louis XIV summoned him to France.   He did an extraordinary bust of the Sun King, which has found its way to the National Gallery in Washington.   The King wanted him to do much more, but in France he met a rivalry as fierce as his own.   He returned to Italy.   It is strange to think that, but for intriguing courtiers, Bernini might have built the Louvre.   It is a pity he did not.   It would have been much less dull than it is.

XIII

A WALK OF DISCOVERY

e have now seen St. Peter's built, twice over. The problem remains of seeing St. Peter's itself, with one's own two eyes, on one's own two feet. It would seem to be a simple matter—a good guide, patience, up the right aisle, down the left, as one does in any great church.

It is not so. Every time after my first few visits to the basilica, I came out onto Bernini's piazza with a distinct feeling of mental indigestion and the beginnings of a headache. There is too much history: it is too diverse. One longs for something more simple, like the Parthenon or Salisbury Cathedral. It is difficult to hurtle through sixteen centuries in an afternoon.

But then I came to live in Rome. I attended the pageant of ceremonies that each year takes place in the basilica. I saw Popes crowned: I saw them buried; I saw them happy: I saw them angry. Each time I went I studied some new aspect of the basilica, taking it piece by piece, at my leisure. I put these pieces together in my mind until one day, at last, I understood the church. I read it, as I have said, like a book.

Before I began this essay, I took two walks around St. Peter's, with my experiences behind me. I shall now describe them.

My first was to Constantine's basilica. As we have seen, it was almost totally destroyed. For that reason, it has a stronger hold on my imagination. In all the avalanche of pictures that we have of St. Peter's, we have only one of the old basilica, and that painted long after it disappeared. So I walked across Bernini's piazza, not looking at it, through Maderno's façade, not worrying about it, down the great church, ignoring Bernini's great theater of the Popes. I came to the end of the church, just before the gesticulating Doctors and the floating Chair. There I found two worn steps, stretching right across the church. They looked so old they made everything else look much too new. They came from the old basilica. Why they survived, nobody knows. Perhaps it was because others had noticed what I did. The two steps were close by the original shrine of St. Peter. On either side there are depressions where the stone has been worn down by the feet of countless pilgrims visiting the holy place. The ruts worn by chariot wheels in the streets of Pompeii move anyone with a sense of history. These two shallow curves are, to me, even more moving. They cannot be stepped on any more. But the pilgrims are still there, shuffling past, in their thousands. This, as much as architects and stonemasons, is what has built St. Peter's.

From there I turned back into the church and went down a flight of stone steps that led me beneath the floor. Here I found a crypt with a semi-circular passage. In the middle of the curve was a narrow chapel, not big enough for four men to stand abreast. At the far end was an altar. Above the altar, dimly lit, was a slab of marble down which ran a vertical band of porphyry. This is the back of the shrine that Constantine built to protect that other shrine which Gaius saw, and which the earliest Christians built over St. Peter's grave.

There is no more telling sight in all Rome. I have seen the spot where Caesar fell at the foot of Pompey's statue, struck down by his assassins. There is no statue. It is a warren of broken brick walls underneath a modern road. Here, seemingly as fresh as when Constantine's masons put it up, is a piece of marble that is a witness to a fact that changed the history of civilization as much, and perhaps far more, than the death of Caesar. I have crouched through a low door in Jerusalem and stood in the Holy Sepulchre, and I did not feel that a single stone I saw was genuine. This is real.

Peremptory notices on the walls pointed to the way out and led me, willy-nilly, to an exit outside the church. The aim of all this is to lead the visitor to a shop selling souvenirs which, with abysmal vulgarity, has been erected in the last bay of Maderno's facade, the one that takes the place of the tower he could not build. Boycotting this (as I trust everybody else of sensibility will), I found the little trick served me very well. It led me to the portico.

Most of its columns look new. But here and there, particularly at the southern end, are columns, some patched, bearing the patina of immense age. They are from classical times. When they were put up, Popes no longer were tearing down Roman ruins for building materials. Therefore, they must have come from the old basilica. They are very Roman, and very noble.

High up in the wall there is yet another relic. Here, in stone, is a decree of Boniface VIII, he who was so nearly killed at Anagni and who began the decline of the Popes that led to Avignon and the ruin of the church I had come to seek. It proclaims the first Jubilee year, and way below it is the sealed door which is opened only for Jubilees. I seemed to hear the tinkle of money as the priests raked it in by St. Peter's shrine.

Near it is another slab bearing a tribute to Adrian I from no less a person than Charlemagne, which led me to go into the church and stand on a large round piece of porphyry in the nave. It was once in front of the high altar in the old basilica. In the year A.D. 800 Charlemagne had come to St. Peter's to hear a Christmas Day Mass. His royal chair stood on the circular stone. At one point (so the story goes) the Pope suddenly produced a crown, and placing it on the astonished Charlemagne's head, proclaimed him to be the Roman Emperor, successor to Augustus and all the rest. The people of Rome, gathered in the nave, shouted their approval.

Charlemagne was undoubtedly crowned on that Christmas Day. The Holy Roman Empire was founded, to plague the Popes for centuries, an institution that has justly been described as neither holy, nor Roman, nor an empire. But it is improbable that Charlemagne was really surprised. There was another Roman Emperor in Constantinople; Charlemagne would scarcely have allowed a Pope to dump a crown on his head without knowing it was going to be done. The act embroiled him with the most powerful monarch on earth, and Charlemagne was a man who calculated his risks. But the stone on which I stood had seen a great day.

The Popes had been given the power to bind or loose, but not to make kings. This they claimed for themselves. They were singularly bad at the job and most of their troubles in the subsequent centuries stemmed from the fact that they insisted on keeping it. They claimed that the right had been given to them by Constantine. Fortunately a Renaissance scholar proved that the document was a forgery. Today the Popes are content with the powers that Jesus gave Peter and the Holy Roman Emperor is no more. All that remains is a great cloak kept in the Pope's private treasury, ready for the Emperor to wear at Mass, should one turn up.

A man of the Renaissance had torpedoed the claim of the Pope to make emperors: the artists of the Renaissance, as we have seen, destroyed the church. But the old basilica, just before it was torn down, carried a most singular monument to its own death sentence, and it is still there, in the new one. The main entrance to the basilica was adorned with two massive bronze doors. They were made by an artist called Il Filarete, and each time I pass them I marvel at their beauty. They show, of course, Peter and Paul. They also show scenes from the Council of Florence, which in 1439 attempted to bring the Latin and the Greek churches together. Like the Council of our own times, it created an enormous stir but in the end did not do anything very much. But there was a new excitement in the air. The Greeks brought with them a profound knowledge of the classics. A passion for antiquity was abroad, and Filarete shared it.

Now one of the things that the medieval Church had abhorred was the religions of the Greeks and the Romans. The chief charge was that the morals of the gods on Olympus were deplorable. Jupiter fell in love, for instance, with a mortal girl called Leda, and seduced her by taking the form of a swan. From a Christian point of view that was disgusting enough, but another exploit of Jove's amounted to a pure abomination. He grew enamored of the pretty young son of a shepherd called Ganymede. Wishing to have him on Olympus as his cupbearer, he changed himself into an eagle, seized the boy in his claws, and carried him off.

Crucifixion of Peter; panel from the bronze doors (Il Filarete, fifteenth century)

LEFT *Bronze doors at main entrance to the basilica (Il Filarete, fifteenth century)*

Filarete surrounded the doors of this most Christian of churches with a border of entwining foliage. In this border he carved a number of little scenes, among them Leda and the swan, and Ganymede and the eagle. All the guidebooks mention the fact, but blushfully fail to point out where this cheeky paganism can be found. Ganymede is the most readily seen. He is about four inches high, and is to be found on the right-hand door, just where a pilgrim would automatically put his hand to push it open. The Christians smashed the statues of the old gods without mercy. But I think there must have been laughter on Olympus when Pope Eugenius IV blessed Filarete's brand-new doors.

There is one other relic of the old church which most of the world thinks was made for the new. Stuck on the side of the basilica was a round chapel devoted to St. Petronilla. It was looked after by the French. An abbot of Cluny, meaning to be buried there, wanted a statue of the dead Christ with the Madonna. He commissioned a young Florentine of twenty-five to do it, stating in the contract, with French preciseness, that it was to be the most beautiful statue in the world. It may be said that he got what he wanted. When the group was set up in the old basilica, it drew all Rome to admire it: and it made Michelangelo Buonarotti a famous young man. The statue was the Pietà.

It is a carving so famous it needs no description, but I would like to point out that I have never really seen it. From the day it left the old basilica and was put in the new one, very few people have. It was designed to be seen at eye-level, so that the spectator could compare the face of the dead Christ and the face of his mother, each echoing the other with unequaled mastery. When it was moved, it was stuck up on a base and the heart of its beauty hidden away. Things were a little better when it was moved briefly to New York. But even there Michelangelo was unlucky. He meant it to be seen close up, in the small chapel for which it was made: in New York the awed public was kept at a distance, on a moving platform. He meant it to be seen in intimate surroundings: the Pietà was displayed in a huge, empty setting conceived by a theatrical designer. The designer, unfortunately, was no Bernini. Now it is back on its perch and a decree has been passed that never again will it leave the Vatican. This is a step in the right direction. Another would be to place it the way that Michelangelo intended. He knew better than Popes, prelates, or Broadway.

OVERLEAF *The Pietà (Michelangelo, 1500)*

XIV

TOMBS AND TASTE

o much for the old St. Peter's: my second visit was to the new. For this I adopted a charming Roman custom. On the great feast days, particularly on that of St. Peter and St. Paul, Roman children are taken to the basilica and introduced to the animals on the tombs of the Popes. The favorites are two lions and their paws have gone quite yellow with the pattings and strokings of small hands. I ignored, therfore, Bernini's great spectacle in bronze, and went around the Papal monuments. They mostly consist of a portrait-statue of the Pope in question, and large figures which symbolize his virtues. But for me the greatest virtue of the Popes is that (as we have seen) they chose the finest artists of their day to work for them. It was a signal honor but also, as I have reasons to know, it could be a signal burden.

137

One evening, at a dinner party in Washington, D.C., I found myself sitting next to the celebrated Italian sculptor Giacomo Manzù. He was a man of small stature and a modest demeanor. The food was excellent, the service without fault, and our host most courteous. Manzù was enjoying himself.

We talked in Italian, through the first course, and Manzù vivaciously described his flattering progress through the States, where he had numberless admirers. The second course was served and Manzù helped himself in the Roman fashion, that is to say, liberally.

Then I spoiled things. I began to talk of Rome. Manzù fell silent. Gloom settled on his face. He put down his knife and fork and stared at his food, no longer eating it. Our host, alarmed, asked him if anything was wrong with what he had been served.

"No, no," said Manzù. "It is my liver. I have lost my appetite."

Now with an Italian, the liver serves as a reason for a whole range of illnesses and discomforts that have nothing to do with it. Manzù was not suffering from a liver attack: he was suffering from an attack of conscience. He explained, still sunk in gloom, with the third course.

"You were talking about Rome," he said to me, "and it made me think of the doors of St. Peter's. Before I left the Pope asked me when they would be ready. They ought to be ready now. But I haven't even begun them."

138

Death in Space, panel from bronze door in the portico (Giacomo Manzù)

From then on nothing could cheer him. He made his excuses, and went home very early.

No artist is always at his best. His abilities come and go with his feelings about the world around him. Bernini, upset about some libelous attacks on him, carved a statue of "Truth" which must be among the worst sculptures in the world. Michelangelo left so much of his work unfinished, not from any romantic theory of art, but because he frequently lost his temper with it and with himself. Bernini's "Truth" is tucked away in a dark corner of a museum. Lesser men can hope that their mistakes will end up forgotten in an attic. The artists that the Popes choose have no such luck, and especially those who work for St. Peter's. What they do, good or bad, will be there to be seen by millions. If it is bad, then their only hope is a bomb, or another Bramante.

The prospect can be paralyzing. Nor is the artist fancy-free. He must please the Pope and to please the Pope he must be in accord with the tastes of the times. The tension may lead to a masterpiece, or it may produce a disaster. In my visit to the tombs of the Popes I saw both. I also saw a fascinating display of what men considered beautiful in these last four centuries.

I began with the tomb of Innocent VIII. It is of bronze and it was made by Pollaiolo, a Renaissance master. It is full of that disciplined elaboration that we admire so much. It was made for the old basilica but so late (1498) it almost belonged to the new. Why it escaped destruction or throwing away we do not know. Certainly it was not because the new man thought it beautiful, as we do. It consists of two parts: above, the Pope sits on a throne; below, he lies on his bier. But when Pollaiolo made it, they were the other way around. The new men clearly thought this was unbearably ugly, so they altered it drastically, nearer to their tastes. It is clear, however, that it was not really the sort of thing they wanted, as I could see from the next tomb I visited.

This was the tomb of Paul III. It is by Guglielmo della Porta, or rather, I should say, by Della Porta in the teeth of Michelangelo. Michelangelo sketched the general idea and then quarreled bitterly with Della Porta about the way it was being carried out. The great man refused to put it where Della Porta wanted it, and it was pushed about the basilica without mercy, losing two of its statues in the process.

Nevertheless, it is very fine. The Pope sits on his throne above (for Pollaiolo's idea had taken the Papal fancy), his hand outstretched in blessing. Justice and Prudence are seated at his feet, but in fact it is a monument to Prudery. The two female figures were once nude, but they have been given robes of tin. For all that, they are beautiful. The whole monument is a sober but successful affair.

I passed to the tomb of Urban VIII. At first sight it looks the same. The Pope is aloft, hand raised in benediction. Two female figures lean on a sarcophagus. But nearly a century has passed between the making of the two monuments. Michelangelo is no longer there to bind the sculptor to his will, or try to. A wind seems to blow around the monument, stirring the draperies. Pope Paul sits in a carved robe, so stiff it seems to be not only of stone, but starched stone. Pope Urban is softly draped, his cloak making a tremulous pattern that commands the eye to follow it. Children peep in and out, and Charity looks at one of them, giving the whole monument a soaring pyramidal line, a line that is challenged, but not defeated, by the angled sword of Justice. And there, between them, a hooded figure of Death is writing an inscription. The whole tomb so bubbles with invention that it makes Michelangelo and Della Porta look prim. It is, of course, by Bernini, and Bernini is showing off. We have seen how he picked up the design of the twisted columns and turned it into the triumph of the baldachino. Here he takes another old design and spins it out into a masterpiece all his own.

He shows off still more in the next tomb I visited. He takes leave of Michelangelo. The sarcophagus has gone. Pope Alexander VII has lost his throne: he does not bless, but kneels in prayer, so brilliantly portrayed that the spectator falls into a respectful silence. A great cloth—but it is of jasper—drapes the door of the tomb, pushed up by a golden skeleton holding a gleam-

Tomb of Innocent VIII (Pollaiolo, 1498)

ing hourglass up to the Pope. Charity and Truth are there, carved with the supreme mastery of marble that Bernini achieved in his old age. And there is, of course, a fine *coup de théâtre*: Truth's left foot rests on a terrestial globe, and is firmly pressed down on Protestant, heretical England.

In these three tombs I had seen the High Renaissance pass into the solemnity of Mannerism, and Mannerism burst asunder to give birth to the Baroque. Those, at least, are the terms that the academies use. But I do not brood on schools: I prefer to use my eyes, rather than my brains. Besides, academies can be a considerable nuisance. The next tomb is a monument to the damage they can do, as well as to Pope Clement XII. There is a kneeling Pope, there are two allegorical figures. But the winds that warmed and stirred the tombs of Bernini had died away. A chill had descended. Looking at the tomb, I often feel I would like to turn up the collar of my coat.

The cause of all this was a German archaeologist called Winckelmann who visited Rome (in 1755) to study antique sculptures. He unfortunately admired them. He had the equipment of a scholar but the temperament of a schoolmaster. The Greeks and the Romans, he laid down, were the *only* people who knew how to sculpt, and everybody must follow them. He drew up the rules, and he would brook no nonsense. Winckelmann can be summed up in one of his own phrases. When a traveler or a young artist approaches a piece of classical sculpture, he said, "he must do so with the certainty that he will find something beautiful. He must keep coming back till he finds it: because beauty is there." If he doesn't find it until school finishes, I presume, Winckelmann could always keep him in when the rest of the pupils go home.

What Winckelmann saw in these statues was a "noble simplicity" and a "quiet grandeur." His books, which are very well written, had an enormous success. Taste changed with remarkable rapidity. The Baroque and Bernini came to be despised. Artists strove to be nobly simple or quietly grand, whereas Bernini and his school were never simple, and although grand, they were never quiet. On the contrary, they always spoke at the tops of their voices. Yet so great was the hold of Winckelmann's ideas on the cultivated public of Europe, that even St. Peter's was held in contempt. The movement soon gave itself a name: the "Neo-classical" style became *de rigueur*. Inevitably, a Pope of the times had to have a Neo-classical tomb. That of Clement XIII was the first, and the most celebrated. The sculptor he chose was the most famous Neo-classicist of them all, Antonio Canova.

When he was young, Canova was a rebel. We all know nowadays that young rebels, sooner or later, are drawn into what we call the System. Canova is a perfect example of how that is done. When he matured, Canova became such a conformist that after he died art historians grew bored with him, or even downright cross. We, in our convulsed modern times, may have more sympathy for him.

Canova was born in a mountain village in the north of Italy, and soon showed signs that he would be a sculptor of genius. He was sent to Venice to learn his trade: there, while still in his early twenties, he made a name for himself.

In 1779 he came to Rome to make his fortune. He did a statue or two that drew attention to himself, and he found a patron. His patron was a connoisseur of art and desperately fashionable in his tastes. Canova was still a country lad, ingenuous to a degree, and unable to speak or write grammatically. He had done little thinking about his art. He loved Nature as a country boy would. He loved human bodies and warm human flesh which his genius helped him translate into marble with a quite remarkable realism.

But this would not do for his patron at all. Canova, he told him, was no longer in the provinces. He was in Rome, a capital city and the fount of fashion. He must learn all about Winckelmann and do his best to carve things the critics would like. He must study the antique.

We have a charming letter in which the young Canova, with terrible grammar and worse spelling, puts down his reaction. He does not want to study the antique, he says. He is quite content to rely on his own gifts. He says he told his patron so, but his patron, soothing him with a cup of chocolate, insisted that he put himself under someone who would teach him all the right and proper things about art. "I do not," concludes the country boy shrewdly, "believe he knows as much about art as he thinks he does."

But he went and studied. There was no alternative. He could not have earned his living if he hadn't, so fierce was the passion for the ancients. He made his statues along the prescribed lines and they were vastly admired. Money and fame came to him. He conformed to the artists' Establishment so well that he became its leader. His manners, his grammar, and his spelling improved with his fame, and he became a man of the world. But the country boy who loved Nature and bodies and flesh was still there, deep inside him. One day it peeped out.

Winckelmann knew a great deal about classical sculpture but there was one thing he did not know. When he enthused about the genius of the Greeks, he was looking, not at Greek originals, but Roman copies. Roman copies were mass-produced. Some were passable: some were bad. Winckelmann thought them all masterpieces. Now a copy is a much colder version of the original; the copyist has not got his heart in it. But it was just this artisan coldness that Winckelmann thought the mark of the Greek genius. All statues, he insisted, had to be cold.

Then Lord Elgin brought the Parthenon statues home to

England.   These, though broken and worn, were genuinely Greek.   Canova, reigning monarch of the Neo-classical School, went to see them.   We have another letter which tells us of his great surprise.   The Greeks, he says, went straight to Nature (as he had done as a boy).   They were not bound by rules; there was nothing rigid about their work.   The works of Phidias, he says, are "true flesh" and thus thoroughly natural.   Then he adds, a little wistfully, "I'm quite proud of my discovery because I have always felt that that is how the great masters must have worked."

The love of the flesh had never left his hand, though it had been buried in his mind.   It is this that should be remembered in front of his monuments.   The figure of Death on the tomb of Clement is a boy, the figure of Religion is a woman.   Both are smooth to excess to get the cold "classical" look that the critics required. But if they are examined more closely and with sympathy, the warm flesh seems to appear underneath the polished surface, as though under a microscopic film of ice.   Once this is discovered, it will be seen how great a sculptor Canova really was.

The art critics have been slow to discover Canova's love of the flesh: but the ordinary uncultured man has found it.   In St. Peter's itself Canova sculpted a monument to the exiled Stuarts, James III, Charles, and Henry.   He carved two angels at the door of a tomb.   The angels are naked, but sexless.   Their androgynous thighs and buttocks are exquisitely carved. The angels are white, except in these parts. Here they have a brown patina from thousands of hands, belonging to visitors, who, no doubt in relief from the solemnity of the place, could not resist the temptation to give the angels a friendly pat.

But the Establishment won. Another young man turned up in Rome, trailing a reputation behind him. He was a Dane called Thorwaldsen, who obeyed all the Neo-classical rules. Canova gave him his blessing and the Pope gave him a commission: the tomb of Pius VII is the last on my list.

I am one of those people who find a certain fascination in a really badly written book, or a thoroughly bad work of art. The creator has always gone to so much trouble to be bad. I am intrigued, too, by the self-satisfaction that oozes from them. From Leonardo da Vinci onward, truly gifted artists have known, and said, that there is always something wrong with a true work of art—something not quite thought out to the end, something given up in despair. Not so with your bad artist. He is always perfectly certain about what he wants to do: he is always sure that it is right, and he always does it, God help us, to the end. Anybody who has attentively studied the English Pre-Raphaelites will know what I mean. The tomb of Pius VII is a perfect example of the genre.

There is the customary figure of the Pope, the door of the tomb,

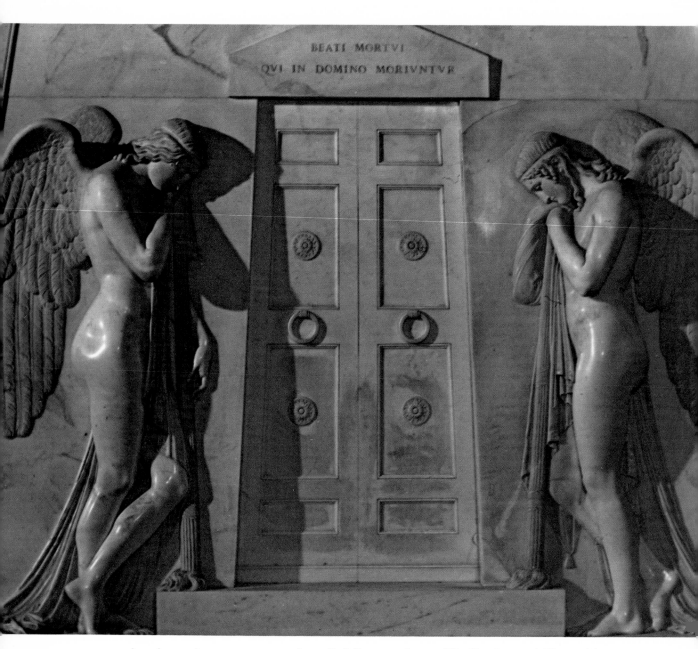

Angels on the monument to the exiled Stuarts, James III, Charles, and Henry (Antonio Canova, 1819)

two of the dead man's virtues, and some angels. The overall design looks as though it has been made with ruler and compasses in some uninspired drawing office. The Pope's face is so stiff he might be in one of those neck clamps that early photographers used to employ. The two figures (I confess I have never troubled to find out what virtues they represent) have that hard-working and hopelessly wrong pose of two girls in amateur theatricals who have to be given parts because their mother is paying for the costumes. The two angels turn their backs on the Pope and contrive to look like two handles of a sugar basin. All is done, of course, in very white, very classical-looking marble.

Nobody liked the tomb when it was unveiled. Thorwaldsen was much criticized, but not for being a bad artist—he had, after all, obeyed all the rules. He was attacked for being a Protestant and for not having his heart in his work. It is curious that a Pope should ask a Protestant to work for him in the first place, but such is the influence of fashion upon the Pontiffs. Thorwaldsen returned to his native Denmark where he died, rich and honored. He is buried under a rose tree in the courtyard of a museum filled with his own works and built with his own money.

Thorwaldsen was not always as bad as he is in St. Peter's. He did some quite passable work that is worth preserving in a museum. But for every person who visits the museum, tens of thousands see the tomb of Pius VII. The world judges him by it, and he is judged to be wanting to the point of absurdity. It cannot were too much for the young incumbent, so he rented them to me. I got to know him and the parish very well and when the archbishop came on his annual visit, I even helped him robe, a business about which he was singularly tetchy.

I then moved to Rome. Now, every two or three years, the parish priest organizes a trip to see the Pope and St. Peter's. Tickets are sold and he takes ten percent for his trouble: and it is a lot of trouble. The pilgrimage is a joyous affair, as full of fun as Chaucer's at Canterbury. Wine and salami are taken aboard the pullman, and a thoroughly merry party arrives in Rome.

They quiet down a little when they stand in St. Peter's Square, but not too much. After all, they are out to enjoy themselves, and they mean to enjoy St. Peter's.

Don Stefano (as I shall call him) takes them around. I have sometimes gone with them. They are still talking and laughing when they go through Filarete's doors (and this I like) but they fall silent in the vast church (for about ten minutes: they will start talking again soon, and this I like to hear even more). They go over to the Pietà. Don Stefano does not talk art with them; he merely says the Virgin looks young because she was a virgin. It was Michelangelo's own defense, but Don Stefano does not know it. He was told the same story when he, a little boy, was taken to see St. Peter's, so he dutifully repeats it. To the pilgrims, the

154

St. Peter's, with the obelisk at the center of the piazza

statue is a picture postcard—the picture postcard that Tonino sent back when he was doing his army service and which, yellowing, is on the wall at home.

He takes them to the baldachino. The women kneel to say a prayer. The men do not. He takes them all on a tour around the bases of Bernini's columns. He points out a small head of a woman on each of them. The heads portray a mother in the stages of childbirth: in apprehension, in agony, and, on the last one, in calm. On this column is the head of a smiling newborn child. The Pope's niece, he tells them, had a difficult parturition when Bernini was putting the baldachino up, and this is a sort of private family joke. It delights the pilgrims: I think it might have pleased St. Peter.

He takes them over to the statue of St. Peter. The women kiss its toes: the men touch it and kiss their fingers. He points to a medallion above it. It shows Pius IX. By a strange tradition each Pope is told at his election that he will not reign as long as St. Peter; that is to say, for twenty-five years. When Pius IX heard it, he said, "That is not an article of faith," which was just as well, for he reigned thirty-two years and was so cock-a-hoop about it, he put up his picture on the wall.

Don Stefano takes them to see the monument to Queen Christina of Sweden. He points out that she is one of the few women allowed to have monuments in St. Peter's, and that she was a Protestant Queen of Sweden who was converted to the Catholic faith, gave up her throne, and came to live in Rome. What he does not say was that her subjects were heartily glad to get rid of her, and paid her a large sum of money to go away. This she did, wearing a pair of men's breeches and calling herself Count Dohna. She wore a skirt for her triumphal entry into Rome, where she set up a lavish establishment which she ruled as a dedicated blue-stocking. Rome, and the Papal court, were amused by her until the money ran out. Then they decided she was a willful, perverse, and boring old woman. She died poor and utterly neglected. The monument was erected as a sort of reparation by the Vatican. But it shows her, cruelly, with an enormous double chin.

Then Don Stefano shows his flock the great porphyry font where, by long tradition, the loose women of Rome can bring an illegitimate baby and have it baptized, with no questions asked. I once stopped to see it happening. The woman gave me such a glare that I fled the church.

Don Stefano and the pilgrims are tired now. On their way out they pass by Manzù's new doors without comment. So shall I. There will be enough in the centuries to come.

ABOVE *Relief from the monument of Queen Christina (Carlo Fontana)*

RIGHT *John XXIII; panel from the bronze door in the portico (Giacomo Manzù)*

XVI

CEREMONIES

Don Stefano's little flock will hear a Mass in St. Peter's. Not all of them: some will be sleeping off the previous night's revels with the deceptively strong Roman wine, because the Mass will be said early in the morning, before the tourists arrive. It is worth getting up to see, for of all the ceremonies in St. Peter's, some of the utmost splendor, this simple little rite is, for me, the most moving.

Any parish priest, however humble, has the right to say a Mass in St. Peter's, provided an altar is free. He presents his documents, and waits his turn. He robes in the huge sacristy and goes out into the nearly empty basilica with two acolytes, who can be (I am told) as trying and cynical as experienced caddies on a famous golf course. His parishioners await him in a side chapel.

The favorite is that of St. Pius X; first, because he was a very simple and holy man, secondly, because he lies in a glass case underneath the altar, in his Papal robes with a metal mask over his face, and that is something to talk about when the faithful get home.

Don Stefano has grown rather hard-bitten about these Masses. But it is moving to watch a young priest saying his first Mass in these awesome surroundings, with his mother, perhaps, a shawl over her head, kneeling in the first pew. It is a common saying among the prelates of the Vatican that what the Catholic Church needs is to go back to the catacombs, meaning, of course, that it needs to recapture the impassioned simplicity of the times of St. Peter and the first Popes. Nowhere has the Church lost this more than in this basilica. But in the early morning, a touch of it is there.

When the Mass is over, the priest blesses his small congregation and dismisses them. They file out of the church and go out on the town for one glorious day until it is time to gather in some piazza and climb aboard the buses for home. As for the priest, he disrobes in the sacristy, goes through a corridor, and—still within the walls of St. Peter's—finds a bar exactly like the one back in his village. It has its advertisements, its neon lighting, its coffee machine, and its row of bottles. He relaxes with a little cup of *espresso*, with perhaps a dash of something strong in it. He needs it.

Someone can be called Blessed or he or she can be made a saint. Only the Pope can do this, and only in St. Peter's can it be done.

Saints or the beatified in these days are usually persons who have founded an Order to do good works among the sick, the poor, orphans, and so forth. The members of these Orders work for years, sometimes for a century or more, to have their founder canonized. They propagandize the Vatican; they collect money for the expenses of the investigation; they gather evidence of miracles that have been worked in the person's life, or after his death. Then, when the great day comes, they pour into St. Peter's, often from the ends of the earth. The basilica puts on gala dress: the columns are hung with tapestries, and extra chandeliers are suspended everywhere. A huge picture of the saint-to-be is hung above the Chair of St. Peter. Special music is composed that is often sung by great choirs drawn from the churches of the Order. Everybody is as happy as they would be at a birthday party, which is what it is, because from now on the saint will have a new birthday (feast day) of his own.

The first part of the ceremony is celebrated in the presence of cardinals in all their glory. Then the Pope comes in on his portable throne, wearing (in the past, and perhaps in the future) his jeweled tiara, in a sign of triumph and rejoicing. He then goes to a praying stool, kneels, and venerates the saint-to-be. He rises and the new saint is proclaimed. The choir bursts into song, the organ peals, and the members of the Order have tears of joy in their eyes. I have seen them embracing one another. It is the greatest day of their dedicated lives.

There is another ceremony peculiar to St. Peter's, and peculiar it certainly is. On the Thursday of the week before Easter, after the Mass, the Sacrament is taken out of the church, and the altars are stripped of their ornaments. The next day, Good Friday, the death of Christ is commemorated in a stark ritual which begins with all the clergy lying prostrate in front of the altar. This takes place everywhere in the world. But only in St. Peter's does the following happen.

A procession is formed, led by a cardinal, followed by bishops, who in turn are followed by the lesser clergy. The procession's tail is made up of the altar boys. All, from the cardinal downward, carry yellow mops. They are just like large household mops, with a big yellow bushy head and a red wooden handle. Oil is poured on the marble top of the altar over the tomb of St. Peter. Then, the cardinal coming first, every member of the procession down to the smallest boy files past the altar and drags his mop across the top as though he is cleaning it.

It is known as the Washing of the Body of Christ, a grim enough name, but the end is charming in a very Italian way. The altar boys run down the steps and greet their families, who are among the few people who have come to watch. Then they make a present of the mop to their mothers or one of their little brothers or sisters, who carry it off home.

As all the world knows, on Sunday at midday during most of the year, the Pope appears at the window of his private apartment and gives his blessing to the crowd gathered below between the arms of the colonnade. This is the ceremony that most foreign visitors see. It is impressive, but it is a trifle formal.

St. Peter's Square sees other benedictions, however, and some are not formal at all. On the occasion of some of the big pilgrimages, the square is turned into a living theatre, something which, I am sure, would have delighted Bernini.

Once I saw it packed with a quarter of a million young people, members of a wide variety of Catholic organizations. They had come to cheer the Pope (who was Pius XII) and to give him an hour-long show. Pope Pius came out on his portable throne and was carried right around the square, waving happily. Another throne had been set up on top of seven steps and under a canopy. There had been some preoccupation for the Pope's health, so, just to show the young people he was still as young as ever he was, he lifted up the skirt of his soutane and ran nimbly up all seven steps, to thunderous applause. He gave a signal for the show to begin.

It took place in the center of the square. Groups did folk dances, young men from the marshes of the French Landes did wonders on enormous stilts, bands played on strange instruments, choirs in bright costumes sang. It is difficult to forget the moment when, after all the movement and noise, a great hush fell over the immense square as the Pope raised his arms to the sky to call down a blessing.

Or again, under Paul VI. While I was writing this essay, I decided one day to take a walk to St. Peter's to check on some fact I had written down. I found the square filled with people from Siena and Assisi and other small villages nearby. Each had brought the town band. Each had brought a team of youths in medieval dress, carrying great banners. Paul VI stood at his window. The bands played as though the musicians would burst their lungs; the youths threw the banners high in the air and caught them dexterously as they came down again. Townsfolk cheered their team. High above it all was the white figure of the Pope, looking much happier than he usually does.

There are times, too, when St. Peter's Square has seen the Pope lay aside all the pomp and circumstance of his office, if only for a few brief minutes. Pope Pius XII found himself in front of tens of thousands of Italian children, come on a pilgrimage to see him. They cheered him when he arrived, and then fell silent with awe. The Pope began his address:

"Are you good children?" he asked them.

"Yes," came a rather wavering answer.

"Do you say your prayers?" asked the Pope.

"Yes," came the reply, a little stronger, but still tremulous.

"Do you eat your spinach?" the Pope demanded.

"*Yes!*" they answered in a delighted roar, and the great façade of St. Peter's echoed with young laughter.

"*The Pope*," say the Romans, "*never fails.*"

XVII

EPILOGUE

We have come a long way together, through sixteen centuries. I have one more story to tell.

One day I was in St. Peter's, reading the large marble plaque on which is carved the names of the Popes who are buried in the basilica. I came across the name of Julius II, the man who had laid the foundation stone of the new church, and who had planned for himself a mighty monument which had never been built. If he were buried in St. Peter's, then, it seemed to me, there must be some monument in the church to record the fact. Yet I could not remember ever having seen one.

I set myself to find it. I searched high and low, but could find nothing. A canon of St. Peter's happened to pass, and I asked him if he knew where Julius's monument might be. He stopped, scratched his head for a while, and then said he thought he did, but wasn't sure.

He took me to an area behind the organ. There was a great pile of benches there; he said we must move them. We worked for fifteen minutes.

There, let into the floor, was a simple tombstone. Julius's name was on it, but not only his. Economically, he had been buried with two of his relatives.

So there he rests, in the humblest tomb in St. Peter's, under a pile of furniture.

Sic transit gloria mundi: and at his coronation, they had told him so.

INDEX